BEYOND THE PROMPT

BUILDING REAL SOLUTIONS IN THE AGE OF AI

Nidhi Mehra

ISBN: 979-8-906060-61-7

First Edition, 2026

Acknowledgement

This book would not have been possible without the unwavering support of my family, whose love and encouragement continue to inspire me every day.

I am deeply grateful to my mentors and peers, whose guidance, insights, and belief in me have shaped the lessons I share here.

To my colleagues and friends, thank you for the conversations that sparked new ideas and for the encouragement that helped me search for clarity. Your curiosity gave this book its direction.

Finally, to every reader who chooses to walk this path: your willingness to learn and grow is the reason these pages exist.

Note to Readers

This book is intended as a practical guide for developers, educators, and leaders navigating the age of **AI**. Its purpose is simple: to help you move beyond the prompt and into building solutions that last.

You will encounter stories drawn from practice, case studies that mirror dilemmas you may face, and checklists you can apply immediately. These are not exhaustive rules but starting points, designed to spark judgment you can carry into your own work.

Think of this section as an orientation rather than a rehearsal: a map of what you will find, not the practice itself. The real rehearsal happens in the chapters, where examples invite you to pause, reflect, and adapt.

While examples and scenarios are based on industry practices, they are meant to inspire ideas rather than prescribe rules. The author and publisher assume no responsibility for errors or omissions, or for damages resulting from the use of the information contained herein.

Preface

This book began in the quiet hours when the office lights had dimmed but the code refused to sleep. A bug in a small feature would suddenly ripple outward, becoming everyone's crisis. Those nights taught me something no manual ever could: judgment is the skill that keeps systems alive when tools fall short.

It is not a language manual or an architecture textbook. It is a guide to the choices we make under pressure, the kind that decide whether a system bends or breaks.

Each chapter offers a rehearsal: a story that shows what can go wrong, a case study that mirrors real dilemmas, and a checklist you can apply immediately. You may read it cover to cover or turn directly to the sections that meet your challenges.

The questions that shaped this book came from colleagues and friends who asked: *How do we make sense of the growing role of* ***Generative AI*** *in our work and lives?* Their curiosity guided its direction, and it is written with gratitude for those voices.

If you carry only one habit forward, let it be this: practice one choice, apply it to one task (ticket), and repeat. Over time, those small, consistent decisions accumulate, turning tidy demos into trusted systems, and late-night fixes into lessons worth sharing.

Table of Contents

Introduction

Every developer knows the feeling: *the rush of a deadline*, the promise of a new tool, the thrill of seeing something work faster than expected. It begins with optimism: the sense that this time, the hard parts might finally be easier. That optimism is real, and it is powerful. But it is also fragile.

After weeks of effort poured into design, code reviews, and endless testing, through late nights, the heated debates, and small victories along the way, everything builds toward one moment: rollout. The team gathers, the plan is set, and the work of weeks or months is finally about to meet the world.

Launch day felt electric. Screens glowed, dashboards lit up, and the team leaned in as the new feature went live. For a moment, everything seemed perfect, the graphs climbed, the demo impressed, and the room buzzed with relief. Speed felt like victory.

But then came another night. A ticket reopened at midnight, alarms filled the channel, and the same team stared at logs that told a harsher story. Fatigue set in, frustration grew, and every "quick fix" unravelled under pressure. What had looked flawless in daylight now revealed brittle seams. Speed had delivered, but judgment had been missing.

This book begins in those moments: the highs that make us believe everything is solved, and the lows that remind us how fragile systems can be. It is written for anyone who has felt both: the thrill of automation and the sting of oversight.

Judgment is not about knowing everything. It is about pausing long enough to ask the questions speed alone ignores: *What assumptions are hidden here? What happens when this grows? Who will rely on this tomorrow?* These questions transform fragile fixes into systems people can trust.

You will not find rigid rules here, but rather rehearsals: stories that reveal what can go wrong, case studies that mirror real-world dilemmas, and habits that compound into credibility. The lessons are not confined to one chapter or one checklist; they are woven through the book, inviting you to practice judgment in every context where speed tempts you to skip it.

AI will always give us speed. But speed without judgment is fragility disguised as progress. Judgment is the craft that makes speed meaningful. It is the bridge between demos and systems, between outputs and outcomes, between code and credibility.

Whether you are a developer, tester, analyst, architect, student, or technology leader, the goal is the same: to build solutions that people can trust. The examples in this book come from software development, but the habits behind them apply wherever technology, people, and decisions intersect.

So let this be your rhythm:

- Pause before you trust.
- Question before you ship.
- Practice judgment until it becomes habit.

Speed fades, but judgment endures.
With foresight, trust is built.
Beyond the prompt lies craft.
And beyond craft lies credibility that lasts.

Part I

Mindset Matters

Chapter 1: Why Prompts Are Not Enough

Magic to Mindset

The cursor blinked on an empty screen. A junior developer watched the **AI** *produce neat, technically correct code samples*, and still felt a knot of doubt. The problem was not syntax; it was direction.

That hesitation is familiar. Every developer, whether new or seasoned, knows the pause when the real question is not ***"Can I write this code?" but "Should I?"*** Execution may be accelerated by **AI**, but deciding what matters remains your responsibility. That decision, the one behind the code, is where the real work begins.

At first, using **AI** feels magical. You type a prompt, "**Add a Download Report button**," and within seconds, **AI** generates a code sample: a button, an endpoint, maybe a CSV export. Quick, clean, correct.

"Prompts may hand you bricks like code samples, tests, scripts in seconds. But without a blueprint, those bricks never form a home."

That speed is a gift and a responsibility. When AI generates runnable code, it hands you bricks; you must supply the blueprint. Prompts produce useful code fragments, but fragments do not carry responsibility. Your job is to translate generated outputs into safe, reliable features by asking the right questions, understanding the broader context, and exercising judgment before those features reach users.

Systems are rarely judged by how quickly code is produced. They are judged by how reliably they behave when real users, real data, and real constraints enter the picture.

Bricks vs Blueprint

Think of **AI** as a brilliant bricklayer: perfectly cut bricks such as code samples, tests, and scripts arrive in seconds. These bricks are useful; they save time and remove tedium. But usefulness is not the same as readiness. A pile of well-made bricks still needs a plan.

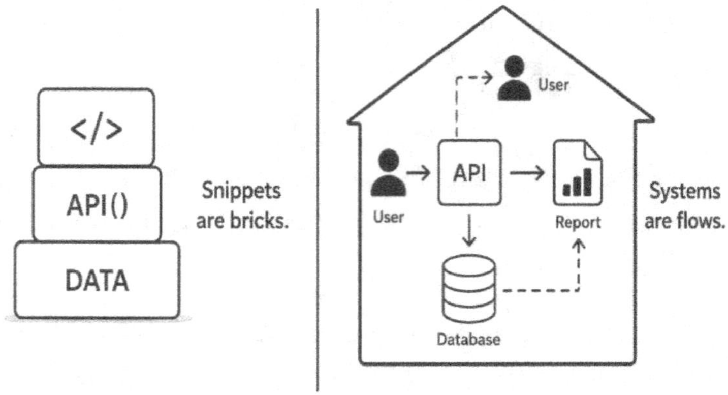

In construction, a blueprint tells you where load-bearing walls go, how plumbing and wiring will run, and where access points and drainage must be placed. Skip any of those decisions and the structure will show its weaknesses later:

leaks, settling, or systems that cannot be extended without major demolition.

Software behaves the same way. A tidy code sample can implement a feature's happy path, but it will not guarantee the feature behaves correctly under real conditions.

Permissions, performance, observability, and edge-case handling are the hidden infrastructure that keep a feature reliable.

Systems thinking is the architect's discipline: it maps how components connect, anticipates stress points, and defines the non-functional requirements that keep a system secure, maintainable, scalable, and resilient. While a code fragment demonstrates how to implement an individual feature, the architectural blueprint reveals how the entire system operates as an integrated whole. That broader perspective is what transforms isolated implementation into a living, adaptable, and dependable system.

Beyond Software

In **data engineering**, a working ETL *(Extract, Transform, Load)* script is a brick; scheduling, retries, and monitoring are the blueprint that keeps the pipeline reliable.

In **event planning**, booking a venue or printing badges are bricks; the master plan that connects logistics, attendee flow, and contingency plans is the blueprint that makes the event seamless.

And in **reporting systems**, exporting CSVs may work well until datasets exceed 1 GB. Without scalability planning, the system can stall or fail under load.

Signals and Safeguards

These are not abstract definitions; they are the signals that reveal system health and the safeguards that prevent fragility. Keep them close; they are the quiet architecture behind every feature.

Visibility & Recovery

- **Observability**: The instruments that let you *see* what is happening (logs, dashboards, alerts).
- **Runbook**: A ready-to-act checklist for what to do when something breaks.

Boundaries & Assurance

- **Permissions**: The guardrails that define who can access or perform certain actions.
- **Acceptance Criteria**: The conditions that prove a feature is complete and trustworthy.

Fragility & Edge Awareness

- **Edge Case**: Rare or unusual inputs that can break the flow (empty data, very large payloads, malformed requests).
- **Encoding**: The rules for representing text correctly (emojis, special characters, multilingual scripts).

These signals and safeguards are not optional extras; they are the invisible supports that turn snippets into systems you can trust.

The Button That Broke

It was a Tuesday afternoon when the product manager dropped a new ticket into the sprint board: "Add a Download Report button." Most developers would knock this out in an hour and move on. That is snippet thinking: solving the local problem without checking the surrounding system.

But the first time the feature went live, small omissions became big problems:

- An analyst tried exporting a large dataset and the system froze.
- A guest user clicked the button and got access to data they should not have seen.
- The finance team complained that the PDF format was missing pagination.

What looked like a small ticket soon rippled across roles, data, performance, and security. The flow that seemed straight forward exposed gaps at multiple handoffs.

User → Button → Endpoint → Export → Database → Logs → Stakeholders

Before you write a prompt to generate a code for: a button, an endpoint or a CSV function, pause and run three quick checks:

➢ **Identify the audience**: who will use this and with what permissions?
➢ **Define the value**: why does this export matter to stakeholders?
➢ **Anticipate failures:** what edge cases, dependencies, and observability needs must we cover?

That shift in mindset is what separates a quick fix from a resilient feature.

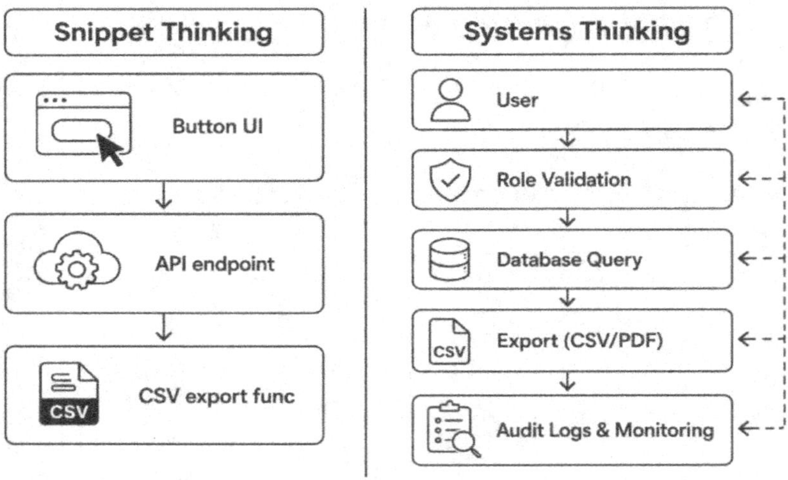

Snippet thinking focuses on fragments. Systems thinking connects them into flows, dependencies, and readiness.

Speed vs Responsibility

Code samples, tests, and boilerplate may be generated in seconds by **AI**, yet the responsibility for design decisions remains yours. Translate those outputs into trustworthy features by pausing for the right questions and quick checks before going live.

Think of these checks as the smallest set of design decisions that turn a working example into production-ready behaviour: identify the audience and intent, enforce permissions, anticipate edge cases, plan for scale, add observability, and document key assumptions. Applying these checks consistently helps prevent small oversights from becoming system-wide failures.

Pair AI's speed with this habit, and you will move from producing tidy code to delivering trustworthy systems.

- Snippets, tests, scripts, boilerplate flows, and quick prototypes may arrive in seconds through **AI**.
- Developers ensure the essentials: context (audience and intent); permissions and security; edge cases (empty results, large datasets, unauthorized users); observability (logs, metrics, dashboards); performance; and usability.

Quick Checklist

- **Audience & intent**: Confirm the user role and the business reason for the feature.
- **Permissions**: Verify server-side authorization and role checks; deny by default.
- **Happy-path smoke test**: Run the feature end-to-end for the expected user and data.
- **Edge cases**: Test empty, very large, malformed, and unauthorized inputs.

- **Performance sanity:** Validate system behaviour under realistic payload sizes and concurrent traffic; apply pagination, caching, throttling, or request limits as required.
- **Observability**: Ensure logs capture failures; add one metric and one alert for critical errors.
- **Error handling and UX**: Confirm user-facing errors are clear and do not leak internals.
- **Dependencies and fallbacks**: Confirm external calls have timeouts, retries/backoff, and graceful fallbacks.
- **Security quick scan**: Check for PII (Personally Identifiable Information) exposure, injection vulnerabilities, access-control gaps, and insecure token handling.
- **Docs and tests**: Add a concise README or code comment, along with at least one automated test covering a critical execution path.
- **Runbook note**: Add one or two immediate remediation steps for on-call.

Think It Through

- What assumption about scale, permissions, or failure modes did you make that **AI** could not see?
- Where does your code sample stop and the system begin?
- Which stakeholder outcome would break first if this feature were stressed?

From Reflection to Action

Goal: Practice writing a context-rich prompt and validating your **AI** output like a system thinker.

1. Pick a recent ticket: Choose something small but real **e.g.,** "Add a Download Report button."
2. Write two sentences
   – Who is the audience? (**e.g.,** admin users, analysts)
   – Why does this matter? (**e.g.,** audit tracking, data export for reporting)
3. **Write a context-rich prompt:** spend 2–3 minutes writing a prompt that includes:
   – User role (who is using it)
   – Data shape (tabular, filtered, paginated)
   – Expected behaviour (formats, error handling, performance expectations)

   Example: "Create a Download Report feature for admin users that exports filtered tabular data as CSV or PDF, supports pagination, and logs each export for audit tracking."
4. Add a short checklist
   – Success criteria (formats, outputs)
   – Permissions (who can use it)
   – Edge cases (empty results, large sets)
   – Dependencies (Database, services, storage)
   – Observability (logs, metrics)
5. **Use AI to generate the code sample**: paste your prompt into your **AI** assistant and review the output. Validate below quickly -:
   – Test one admin and one viewer
   – Check empty and large result sets
   – Confirm both CSV and PDF outputs

6. **Write one sentence**: what did the **AI** miss? Add it to your notes or checklist.

Prompts give you bricks; only you can supply the blueprint. Name the audience, clarify why the feature matters, and anticipate edge cases, that is how fragments become outcomes. A tidy code sample may run once, but a resilient feature *requires permissions, performance planning, observability, and clear failure paths*.

Code samples get you started; systems earn trust, scale, and longevity. *And that is the next step: learning how bricks connect into houses, and how snippets connect into systems*.

Chapter 2: Thinking in Systems, Not Snippets

From Connections to Systems

The whiteboard was crowded with sticky notes: buttons, endpoints, exports. Each snippet was neat, correct, complete in isolation. Yet the system felt incomplete. How would data flow between modules? What happened if one service failed?

That pause mattered. Snippets solve fragments, but systems solve reality. Fragments arrive quickly through **AI**; systems emerge only when you connect them with foresight. Prompting well is a skill, but prompts shape outputs, not outcomes. A clever prompt may generate a neat snippet, yet it will not anticipate ripple effects, dependencies, or failures.

Your value lies in systems thinking: understanding how snippets connect to databases, APIs, users, and infrastructure, and how they behave under stress. Without this mindset, even well-written code can fail when placed inside a real-world system.

Systems thinking means anticipating how each part behaves, connects, scales, and recovers. The six lenses introduced in this chapter provide a practical framework for examining software systems from multiple perspectives.

These lenses are not abstract ideals; they are everyday checks that influence architecture decisions, development practices, testing strategies, deployment planning, and troubleshooting activities. Throughout the remainder of this book, they will serve as a recurring guide for evaluating how systems behave, evolve, and respond to change in real-world environments.

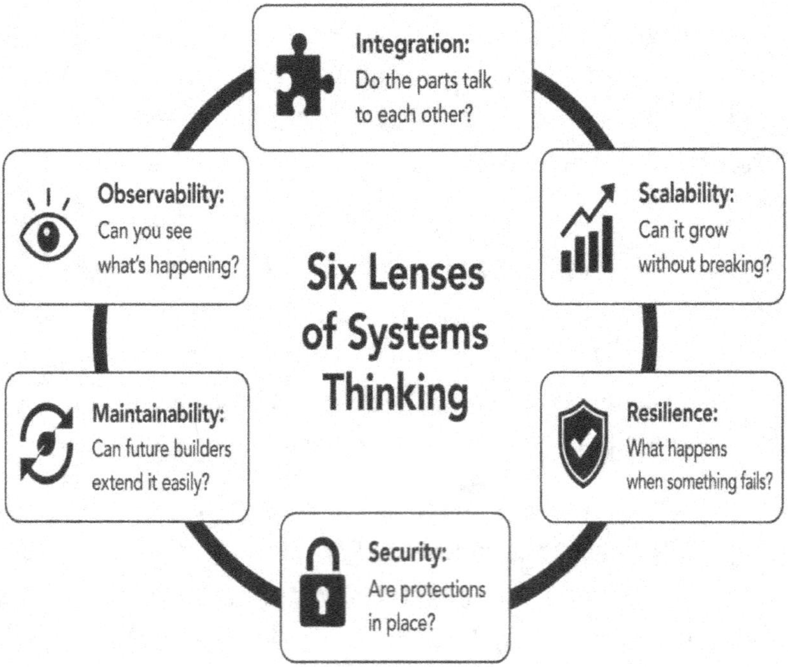

Design Trade-offs in Practice

Systems thinking is not just about spotting what is missing, it is about weighing what you gain against what you give up. Each lens carries its own tension:

- Integration makes features flow seamlessly, but tighter coupling means a single failure can ripple outward.

- Scalability prepares you for tomorrow's growth, yet building for scale too early can add cost and complexity before demand arrives.
- Resilience improves uptime with retries and fallbacks, but overuse can hide deeper issues or slow responses.
- Security protects users and data, though stronger safeguards often increase friction and support overhead.
- Maintainability ensures future developers can extend the system, but modularity and abstraction can slow initial delivery.
- Observability speeds debugging with rich telemetry, but too much data can overwhelm teams and inflate storage costs.

Trade-offs are not flaws; they are the reality of systems. The skill lies in choosing which tension to embrace, and when, so your design remains balanced under real-world pressure.

Built to Last

An owner buys a plot and secures blueprint approval. During the review, the owner does not simply check room sizes and setbacks; they imagine morning coffee steaming in the kitchen, a bicycle resting beside the back door, and a storm that will eventually test every seam of the structure.

The owner asks the builder to install additional conduits behind the walls so future lighting, sensors, or controls can be added without tearing the house apart. They ask the electrician to label every circuit clearly so that even a stranger can locate the correct breaker at midnight. These small, deliberate decisions are more than construction details; they are promises about how the house will behave when people, weather, and time place pressure on the system.

On a wet afternoon, the sump pump fails. Because the house was designed for failure, a secondary pump activates automatically, and a simple valve reroutes the flow until the primary unit is repaired. A neighbour who minimized upfront costs watches water creep across the floor; the homeowner monitors the control panel and calls the technician before the carpet begins to warp.

Later, when a delivery service changes its protocol and the smart lock no longer recognizes access codes, the labelled wiring and accessible service panel allow a repair that might have taken a week to be completed in a single afternoon.

The house does not endure because it is beautiful; it endures because the team anticipated how systems connect, how they might fail, and how to detect the earliest signs of trouble.

The systems integrator on site installs the conduits, wires the control panel, and verifies that the plumber's valves, the electrician's circuits, and the alarm system all communicate correctly. This hands-on work is the moment where plans become a living system: interfaces are reconciled, adapters are fitted, and instrumentation is placed so the earliest signs of drift appear as clear, actionable signals.

Before you continue, answer these two prompts and add the responses to your sketch:

1. Build now for change (by accepting modest upfront cost) or optimize for the cheapest launch (and plan to retrofit later)?
2. Which single instrument will you add that, when it moves, forces action? Label it on your sketch.

Then, without naming roles, run the six lenses over your design: how does this piece link to the system; can it grow without tearing everything apart; what happens when a dependency fails; what keeps people and data safe; can a future hand repair or extend it; and what single signal will tell you something is drifting wrong?

Answering these questions transforms a neat implementation into a system designed to endure.

Beyond Software

Systems thinking applies everywhere, not just in code. Imagine setting up a **coffee shop**:

- **Integration**: The cashier, barista, and supply chain must coordinate. If the cashier forgets to pass the order, the barista will not make the drink.
- **Scalability**: Can the shop handle a morning rush of 100 customers? Without extra staff or faster machines, the system collapses under peak demand.
- **Resilience**: What if the espresso machine breaks, is there a backup? A spare machine or alternate menu keeps the shop running.
- **Security**: Are payments handled safely? If the cash drawer is left open or card data is not protected, trust is lost.

- **Maintainability**: Can new staff learn the workflow quickly? Clear instructions and simple processes keep operations smooth.
- **Observability**: Does the manager have a dashboard to track sales, stock, and wait times? Without visibility, the shop runs blind, stock runs out, queues grow, and problems go unnoticed.

Just like a shop that faces bottlenecks and frustrated customers during a morning rush without enough staff or equipment, software systems falter under heavy load when scalability is ignored.

Whether you are wiring a house or running a coffee shop, the same lenses apply. Systems thinking is not confined to code, it is a way of seeing how parts connect, scale, fail, and recover in any domain. That is why developers must learn to think beyond snippets: the mindset travels with you, wherever systems exist.

Invisible Connectors

These are not just definitions; they are the unseen links that hold systems together. Each one is a connector: invisible when things run smoothly, but essential when fragments strain under growth, failure, or attack.

Trust & Accountability

- **Authentication**: Confirms someone is who they say they are.
- **Audit Trail**: A record of what happened, like a logbook.

Growth & Recovery

- **Scalability**: The ability to grow without breaking.
- **Resilience**: The ability to recover quickly when something fails.

Load & Flow Control

- **Rate Limiting**: Restricts how often an action can be performed to prevent overload.
- **Retry with Backoff**: Retries failed operations with increasing delays to avoid overwhelming a service.
- **Circuit Breaker**: A safeguard that stops repeated failing calls to protect downstream systems.

These invisible connectors are the quiet forces of systems thinking: the signals, safeguards, and feedback loops that transform isolated snippets into designs built to endure.

Practice Arena: Turning Snippets into Systems

A new ticket appears in the backlog: "Add Forgot Password functionality." At first glance, the request seems straightforward. A user clicks a link, enters an email address, receives a reset token, and creates a new password. It is the kind of feature users rarely notice when it works well, but quickly miss when it does not.

The developer reviews the request and begins sketching the flow. Nothing about it appears particularly complex. Yet experience has taught them that seemingly simple features often become more complicated once real users, real traffic, and real failures enter the picture.

The developer opens the editor, ready to begin. This is the kind of task where **AI** feels useful: a quick prompt, a clean snippet, a working starting point. Within seconds, a tidy flow appears: authenticate the user, generate a reset token, and send it by email. On the whiteboard, the diagram looks complete.

But as the marker squeaks across the board, the developer pauses. Something feels unfinished. The snippet is clean, but what happens when hundreds of users click the link at the same time? What happens if the email provider slows down or fails entirely? What prevents reset tokens from lingering indefinitely?

The questions are no longer about the code itself; they are about the system the code must survive within.

Integration

The reset flow must talk to the authentication service, the database, and the email provider. The developer imagines the email service failing mid-request. Without logging and graceful exit, the system would leave users confused. So, they add an audit trail, ensuring even failed attempts are recorded.

Your Turn: Sketch the flow:

User → Authentication Service → Database → Email Provider

- If the email provider fails, what fallback would you add?

Once the pieces start talking to each other, the next question emerges: can they still keep pace when the conversation grows louder?

Scalability

What if 1,000 users click "Forgot Password" during a breach scare? The snippet alone would hammer the database and email queue. The developer sketches a rate limiter and a durable queue, knowing these add latency but prevent collapse under load.

Your Turn: Imagine a sudden spike.

- Would you choose rate limiting per IP or queuing with backoff? Why?

Growth brings pressure, and pressure reveals cracks; now the developer must ask how the system behaves when something gives way.

Resilience

Tokens expire, providers go down, IDs are invalid. The developer rehearses each failure mode: retry with backoff for transient outages, fallback messages for expired tokens, clear exits for invalid IDs. Each safeguard is a promise that the system will not crumble when reality intrudes.

Your Turn: Pick one failure mode (e.g., expired token).

- What message should the user see?
- Should the system retry, fallback, or exit?

Surviving failure is one thing; surviving attack is another. The developer shifts from recovery to protection.

Security

The snippet from **AI** does not enforce one-time use or expiry. The developer sets a 15-minute lifetime, encrypts the link, and blocks brute force attempts. They weigh convenience against protection, knowing frustrated users are better than compromised accounts.

Your Turn: Choose a token lifetime: *15 minutes, 1 hour, 24 hours.*

- Which balances security and usability best for your context?

With safeguards in place, attention turns to longevity; how future builders will inherit and extend what has been created.

Maintainability

The developer thinks of the teammate who will debug this flow a year later. Modular components, clear naming, and documentation become part of the design. The snippet grows into a structure that future hands can extend without fear.

Your Turn: Look at a snippet you have written before.

- Could another developer understand it in 30 seconds?
- If not, what naming or comments would help?

A system that lasts must also be seen clearly. The developer moves from building stability to building visibility.

Observability

The developer imagines dashboards that look fine but hide silent failures. They add metrics: reset requests per minute, email delivery success, token expiry distribution. Alerts trigger when spikes suggest an attack or when delivery rates dip below baseline. Visibility turns fragility into foresight.

Your Turn: Pick one metric to track.

➢ What threshold would force you to act immediately?

Observability Metrics Callout

To make the reset flow visible and trustworthy, track:

➢ **Reset requests per minute**: alert on abnormal spikes.
➢ **Email delivery success rate**: alert if success drops below baseline.
➢ **Database pool utilization**: alert if sustained usage exceeds safe thresholds.
➢ **Token expiry distribution**: ensure tokens are being used or expiring as expected.

These metrics turn observability into actionable practice, helping you catch issues before users notice.

Trade-offs in Action

Short token expiry improves security but frustrates users when links expire too quickly. Queuing improves scalability but adds latency. Retries improve resilience but can mask deeper failures.

These tensions are inherent to systems; the skill lies in choosing which to embrace, and when.

Flow in Practice

The flow now reads not just as code, but as a living system:

➢ Success path: generate → store → email.
➢ Failure path: log → exit → alert.

The diagram below shows how the same forget password feature, that can be viewed through multiple systems-thinking lenses. Rather than focusing only on functionality, it highlights how integration, security, scalability, maintainability, observability, and resilience shape the behaviour of the system in production. Each lens reveals a different set of risks, trade-offs, and design decisions that influence the overall user experience.

Blind spots remain: no rate limiting, tokens that never expire, dashboards that mask errors. The developer learns that systems thinking is not a checklist but a lens applied continuously.

AI vs Human Judgment

- Fragments may be accelerated by **AI**, but foresight belongs to you.
- Queries might be scaffolded by **AI**, yet thresholds and trade-offs are human judgment.
- Happy-path prototypes emerge quickly through **AI**, but resilience is designed by you.
- **From responsibility to foresight:** Human judgment not only checks permissions and edge cases, but also spots anomalies across systems, anticipates ripple effects, and designs observability strategies that keep the system honest under stress. It is the shift from reacting to issues, toward shaping systems that endure under growth, failure, and attack.

That judgment turns a snippet into a reliable system. The Forgot Password flow looks simple in code, but only systems thinking makes it reliable in production. Each lens adds foresight. Each trade-off is a choice. Each blind spot is a reminder: snippets run, but systems last.

Think It Through

Before you act, pause and think: When **AI** gives you a snippet, do you pause to ask: *"How does this fit into the system?"*

- Think of the Forgot Password example: which parts would **AI** generate, and which parts require your judgment?
- What failure modes can you anticipate in your own projects?
- How would you add observability so you can *see* what is happening when things go wrong?
- Are you designing for today's user load, or tomorrow's growth?
- Which **trade-offs** are you willing to accept in your design, and why?

From Reflection to Action

Pick a small feature you have built (like a login, search bar, or API call).

1. **Prompt AI** to generate the basic snippet.
2. Then, for each lens of systems thinking, ask yourself:
    – What other services must this connect to?
    – How will it behave with 1,000 users at once?
    – What happens if a dependency fails?
    – How do you protect against misuse?
    – Can future developers extend this easily?
    – How will you monitor and debug it in real time?

3. Sketch a quick diagram of the flow, labelling where each lens applies.
4. Compare your system design to the raw snippet **AI** gave you: notice where foresight, not code, makes the difference.

Systems thinking is the bridge between what **AI** can generate and what developers must design. Snippets are useful, but they remain incomplete until they are connected into a larger framework. When you consider integration, scalability, resilience, security, maintainability, and observability together, a feature becomes part of a living, reliable system.

Systems thinking is not a checklist you tick once; it is a continuous lens applied to every feature, every design, every decision. ***AI*** *accelerates the work, but you provide the judgment, foresight, and responsibility that make systems real. That is the difference between code that runs and systems that last.* Let's see how these lenses apply in a real feature: not as theory, but as a lived experience.

Case Study: Reporting Dashboard

It started with a simple request: *"Add a reporting dashboard so managers can track performance."*

On the surface, it looked straightforward: a page with charts, filters, and export options. **AI** quickly generated chart components, database queries, and a scaffolded layout. Within hours, a prototype was ready.

But when the dashboard went live, hidden issues surfaced in the system:

- The charts froze when datasets grew beyond a few thousand rows.
- One service outage caused the entire dashboard to fail.
- Sensitive financial data was visible to users without proper permissions.
- Errors were happening silently, with no logs or alerts to show what was wrong.

These failures mirror the blind spots we saw earlier: snippets that looked fine in isolation but collapsed when placed inside a system.

The dashboard was not just a collection of charts; it was an interconnected system of users, data, services, permissions, and dependencies. And interconnected systems demand more than isolated code samples.

What AI Prompting Handled Well:

AI handled much of the initial dashboard implementation:

- ➢ Chart components (e.g., bar, line, pie)
- ➢ Database queries for pulling records
- ➢ Export functions (CSV, PDF)
- ➢ Layout scaffolding with filters and tabs

The diagram below illustrates the dashboard flow and highlights the key system lenses that help evaluate it.

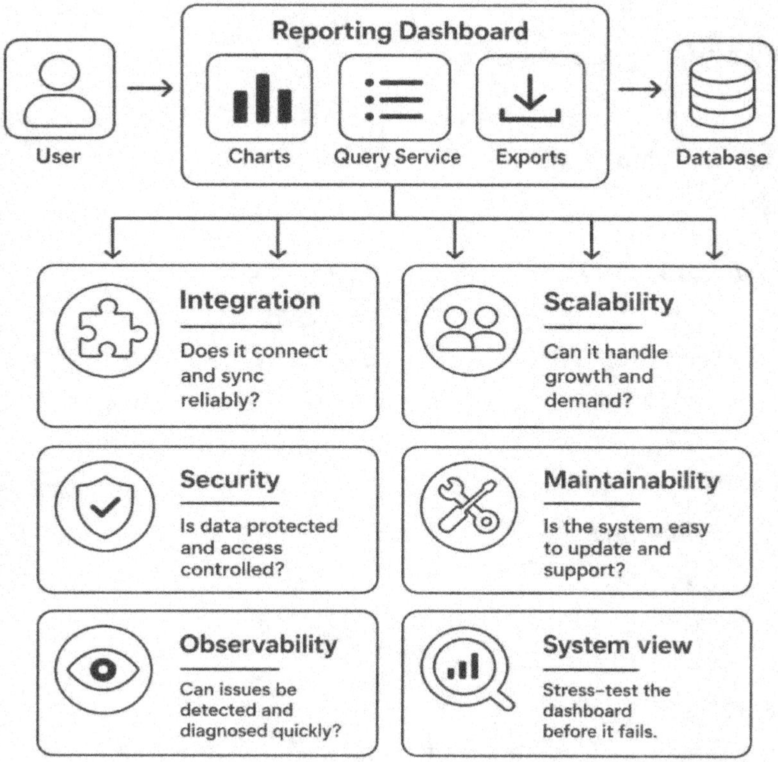

While these capabilities provide a strong starting point, they address only the visible aspects of the solution. The generated code did not consider how the system would behave under user load, data growth, failure, change, or operational pressure.

Systems thinking encourages us to examine the entire flow rather than individual features. A reporting dashboard may appear simple on the surface, but it relies on multiple interacting components: users, queries, charts, exports, and databases. Each component introduces architectural questions that AI-generated code alone may not answer.

Applying Six Lenses

Each lens exposes a different risk. Pause at each one, ask the question honestly, and consider what could fail if you ignore it.

- **Integration**: Do the filters, queries, and exports align across services, or are they stitched together loosely? If they are stitched together loosely, you will see mismatched results: filters applied incorrectly, exports missing data, or charts displaying stale information. Integration means designing flows *so every part speaks the same language.*
  Try this:
  Add a contract test that validates filter → query → exported result shape.
- **Scalability:** What happens when managers query millions of records instead of thousands? Without pagination,

caching, or optimized queries, the dashboard freezes. Scalability means planning for growth before it arrives, so performance holds steady under load.

Try this:

Enable pagination on the query and add a lightweight cache for repeated heavy requests.

- **Resilience:** If the analytics API fails, does the dashboard crash or recover gracefully? Without resilience, one outage takes down the whole system. With resilience, you show a fallback message and retry intelligently, so the dashboard remains usable even under stress.

  Try this:

  Add a user-facing fallback and a retry with backoff for analytics calls.

- **Security:** Are exports respecting permissions, or can anyone download sensitive data? If permissions are not enforced, confidential information leaks. Security means enforcing role-based access and safeguards that protect both the system and its users.

  Try this:

  Enforce a server-side role check before returning any export payload and log the export.

- **Maintainability:** Will future developers be able to extend the dashboard without tearing it apart? If code is tangled, every change risks breaking something. Maintainability means modular components, clear documentation, and consistent naming so the dashboard evolves smoothly.

Try this:
Refactor one chart into a reusable component and add a two-line README describing its props and data contract.

- **Observability:** Are failures visible through logs and alerts, or do they stay hidden until users complain? Without observability, problems remain invisible until trust is lost. Observability means logs for query failures, dashboards for latency, and alerts for unusual spikes.
  Try this:
  Log export attempts, track query latency, and create an alert for export failure rate > 2% over 5 minutes.

Viewed individually, each lens highlights a specific risk. Viewed together, they provide a practical framework for evaluating whether a feature is ready for the real world. A dashboard that satisfies all six lenses is more likely to remain useful, trustworthy, and maintainable long after its first release.

Trade-offs in Action

Pagination improves scalability but adds implementation complexity. Role checks improve security but may introduce additional user friction. Retries improve resilience but can sometimes hide deeper operational issues. Every safeguard carries a trade-off. Systems thinking is the discipline of recognizing those trade-offs and balancing them deliberately so the system remains effective under real-world conditions.

From Reflection to Action

Using the prototype **AI** gave you, pick the export flow and apply the six lenses in one pass:

1. Add the contract test
2. Enable pagination and caching
3. Add a fallback UI and retry logic
4. Enforce a server-side permission check
5. Refactor a component and document it
6. Add one metric plus an alert.

Run the flow and write one sentence about what the system revealed that the snippet did not.

Try this next time: *Before your next pull request (PR), pause, name who uses the feature, list the single most likely failure, and apply one lens to address it.* Do that consistently and your snippets will stop being fragile and start becoming systems people can trust.

Closing Thoughts

Prompts spark momentum, but systems sustain progress.

AI can accelerate your work, yet only systems thinking prevents silent failures and earns trust. The shift from coder to problem solver comes through habits: pausing for context, anticipating ripple effects, checking dependencies, and planning observability.

You have seen the consequences when these habits are missing: a button that broke, a password reset that failed silently, a dashboard that exposed weaknesses. Each one proved that snippets alone cannot carry production.

Snippets may start the journey, but systems carry it forward; resilient, secure, and observable.

Carry this mindset *into Part II, where we will connect these habits to the Software Development Life Cycle and see how they scale from single features to the rhythm of an entire team*

Part II *Software Development Life Cycle (SDLC)*

Chapter 3: The Rhythm of the SDLC

From Steps to Rhythm

The bug was small, almost invisible. A missing check in the code meant the system crashed when a rare input appeared. Automated tests had passed, the release went live, and the team celebrated. Two weeks later, a frustrated user uncovered the flaw: a crash no one had anticipated.

It was not the code itself that was the problem; it was the skipped step. Testing had been treated as a checkbox, not a safeguard. The rhythm of the SDLC had collapsed.

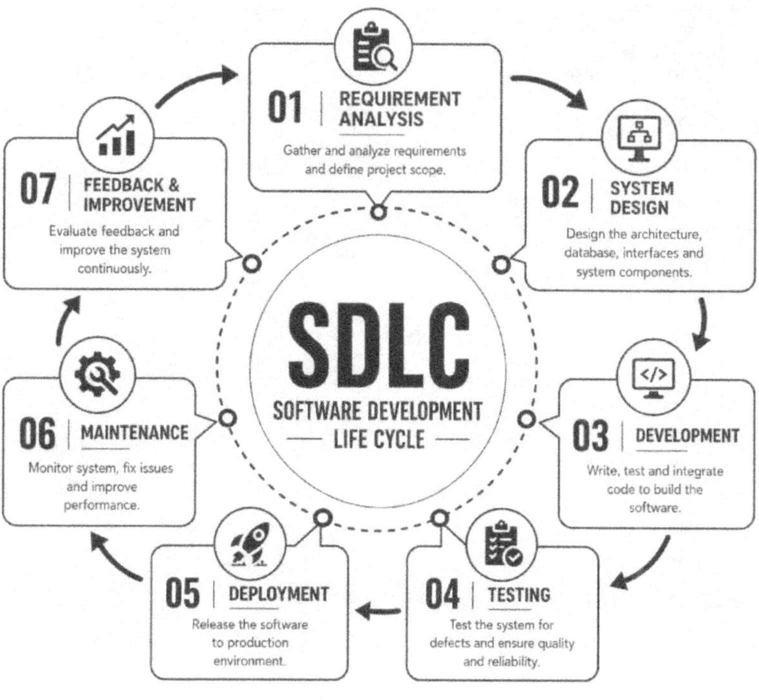

Every team has a rhythm. Builders follow blueprints, chefs follow recipes, musicians follow scores. Software teams follow the SDLC (Software Development Life Cycle): not because it is paperwork, but because it provides structure, coordination, and feedback throughout delivery. Skip a step, and the dance stumbles.

Two Worlds, One Rhythm

Think of building software like building a house. You decide how many rooms you need, sketch the blueprints, lay the bricks, inspect the wiring, hand over the keys, and keep fixing leaks. Skip inspection or ignore upgrades, and the house may look fine at first, but it will not stand strong for long.

Or picture planning a wedding. From choosing the guest list to walking down the aisle, each step mirrors the SDLC. Skip the rehearsal or the tasting, and the big day suffers.

Stage	***Building House***	***Wedding Planning***
Requirements	Decide how many rooms and their purpose	Choose the guest list and style
Design	Create blueprints, plan plumbing and wiring	Pick the venue, hire a florist
Development	Lay bricks, install systems	Hire a caterer, DJ, photographer

Testing	Inspect doors, water flow, electricity	Have a dress rehearsal
Deployment	Hand over the keys	Walk down the aisle
Maintenance	Fix leaks, upgrade wiring, add new rooms	Write thank-you notes, celebrate anniversaries

Beyond Software

The SDLC is not unique to coding; it is the same rhythm you see in everyday projects.

Think about **opening a restaurant**: requirements are deciding the cuisine and target customers, design is laying out the kitchen and dining area, development is training staff and setting up equipment, testing is the soft opening, deployment is the grand opening night, and maintenance is updating menus and repairing equipment. Miss the soft opening, and you risk chaos on opening night.

Or think about **planning a family trip**: requirements are deciding the destination, budget, and travel dates; design is booking flights, hotels, and activities; development is preparing by packing bags and arranging documents; testing is double-checking tickets, confirming bookings, and making sure passports are ready; deployment is travel day itself, boarding the plane and starting the adventure; and maintenance is sharing photos, reflecting on the trip, and adjusting plans for the next journey. Miss the testing step, and you risk arriving at the airport only to discover your flight was booked for the wrong day.

Invisible Anchors

These are not just words; they are the anchors that hold the rhythm of the SDLC together. Each one is a stage that may feel invisible in the rush of delivery, but without them, systems collapse under pressure.

Planning & Design

- **Blueprint (Requirements)**: The plan before you build; without it, you do not know what to create.
- **Architecture (Design)**: The structure that ensures everything fits together; without it, systems collapse under pressure.

Building & Verification

- **Construction (Development):** The actual building or coding work; without it, ideas never become real.
- **Inspection (Testing)**: The check before you trust; without it, flaws reach the user.

Delivery & Care

- **Move In (Deployment)**: The moment users or guests step inside; without it, the product never reaches people.
- **Upkeep (Maintenance)**: The care that keeps things working; without it, systems decay over time.

These invisible anchors are the rhythm of the SDLC: the quiet stages that transform ideas into systems, and systems into lasting solutions.

From Request to Reality

Imagine the request lands on your desk: *"We need performance tracking in our app."* It sounds straightforward, just add metrics. But as you walk through the SDLC, you realize each stage asks a different kind of question. Speed alone will not answer them. *What matters is the pause, the judgment, the foresight.*

Requirements - Pause and Plan

You stop before writing a single line. What decision will this metric help someone make? A dashboard full of page views might look polished, but it will not help a manager who cares about response times or error rates. Choosing the right metric is less about speed and more about empathy. User stories may be summarized by **AI**, even draft acceptance criteria, but only you decide what matters.

Try this: *Write one clear acceptance criterion and list two non-functional constraints, like privacy compliance or latency.*

It is like planning a restaurant menu. **AI** can suggest dishes, but only you know what guests actually want to eat. That pause is your blueprint.

Design - Flows and Fault Lines

Wireframes and diagrams begin to take shape. The question is not just *how* it looks today, but *how* it will hold tomorrow. Will the design scale when traffic doubles? Will it stay secure when compliance rules change? A neat diagram today can become tomorrow's bottleneck if you do not plan ahead. Diagrams might be sketched or patterns suggested by **AI**; you choose where the stove goes so staff can move safely.

Try this: *Sketch the flow of data from user action to storage, marking one point of failure and one security check.*

Development - Cooking the Code

Now the coding begins. Boilerplate flows easily, but the happy path is not enough. What happens when the dataset explodes? Or when permissions fail? If you do not plan for failure, bugs slip into production unnoticed. Boilerplate and test cases flow quickly through **AI**; foresight, however, is yours alone.

Try this: *Write one "failure first" test before the success case. It feels slower, but it is foresight that keeps systems reliable.*

It is like cooking. **AI** can prep ingredients, but only you taste and adjust seasoning.

Testing - Taste Before You Serve

Automated scripts run smoothly, but they do not notice if the interface confuses a tired user at midnight. Without empathy, testing misses the human edge cases. Load simulations may come from **AI**, yet only you notice when the soup is too salty.

Try this: *Run one manual test as a frustrated user: take an unexpected path, enter unusual data, see what breaks.*

Deployment - Opening Night

The feature is ready to ship. Pipelines are drafted; logs are monitored. But before hitting "go," you pause. What if something goes wrong? Without a rollback plan, one bug could take down the system. Pipelines may be automated by **AI**, but the safety net is planned by you.

Try this: *Write down the rollback command or deployment reversal steps before release. It is simple, but it is the safety net that makes you confident to ship.*

It is like opening night at a restaurant. **AI** can set the table, but you plan for what happens if a dish runs late.

Maintenance - Preserving Intent

Months later, another developer extends the feature. Optimizations appear, anomalies are flagged, but intent is not obvious. Without context, maintenance becomes guesswork. **AI** may suggest optimizations, but only you can decide when a change is worth the operational cost and risk.

Try this: *Add a brief comment explaining why the logic exists, not just what it does. That clarity turns upkeep into trust.*

"Speed ships features. Foresight sustains them. The pauses, choosing the right metric, sketching secure flows, writing failure tests, testing like a frustrated user, planning rollback, documenting intent, are where your value shines. Snippets may spark progress, but systems carry it forward. That is not acceleration; that is craftsmanship."

Think It Through

- *Am I using **AI** to accelerate my thinking, or to avoid it?* Skipping this reflection risks outsourcing judgment; the very skill that makes you valuable.
- *Which SDLC stage do I naturally take ownership of and which one do I tend to skip?* Ignoring this can leave blind spots, where failures creep in unnoticed.
- *How do I check that **AI**'s outputs align with system goals, not just quick wins?* Without this pause, you risk shipping features that look good but miss the mark.
- *What is one decision I made recently that **AI** could not have made for me and why was it uniquely human?* Forgetting this reflection erodes confidence in your own judgment.

From Reflection to Action

Take a recent feature you worked on and walk it through the SDLC.

1. Map it across the six stages.
2. At each stage, jot down:
   – What **AI** could have done.

– What I needed to do myself.

3. Highlight the moments where judgment, empathy, or foresight made the difference.

This exercise is not about proving **AI** wrong; it is about noticing where your value shines brightest.

*You have now seen how **AI** fits into the rhythm of the SDLC. But teams do not all dance the same way. Some move step by step in **Waterfall**, others improvise in **Agile**. Each approach changes how you think, how you plan, and how you collaborate. In the next chapter, we will explore how your mindset shifts depending on the choreography your team follows.*

Chapter 4: The Choreography of Development

From Rhythm to Choreography

The meeting room was still, broken only by the hum of laptops. A launch had failed, not because the code was faulty, but because the team's rhythm was. Requirements froze months earlier, designs lagged, and development marched forward like clockwork. By the time testing revealed the flaw, that the "performance tracking" feature measured the wrong metric, the release date was already locked. The system looked polished, but it answered the wrong question.

This was not an isolated misstep. Teams everywhere face the same dilemma: projects delivered on time, yet missing the mark. Sometimes requirements are locked too early, leaving no room for change. Other times iteration runs unchecked, producing endless versions without coherence. In both cases, the choreography falters.

Software development is not just about stages; it is about the choreography between them. Some teams move in strict sequence, step by step, with carefully defined handoffs. Others adapt continuously, adjusting to feedback through rapid iterations. Many combine elements of both, creating an approach tailored to their context.

The choice of methodology matters. It decides whether your system stumbles under pressure or adapts gracefully to change.

Once you understand the SDLC stages, the next question is: *How do teams organize this cycle?* Two dominant approaches are **Waterfall** and **Agile**. Each has strengths, limitations, and unique ways **AI** may accelerate or support these approaches.

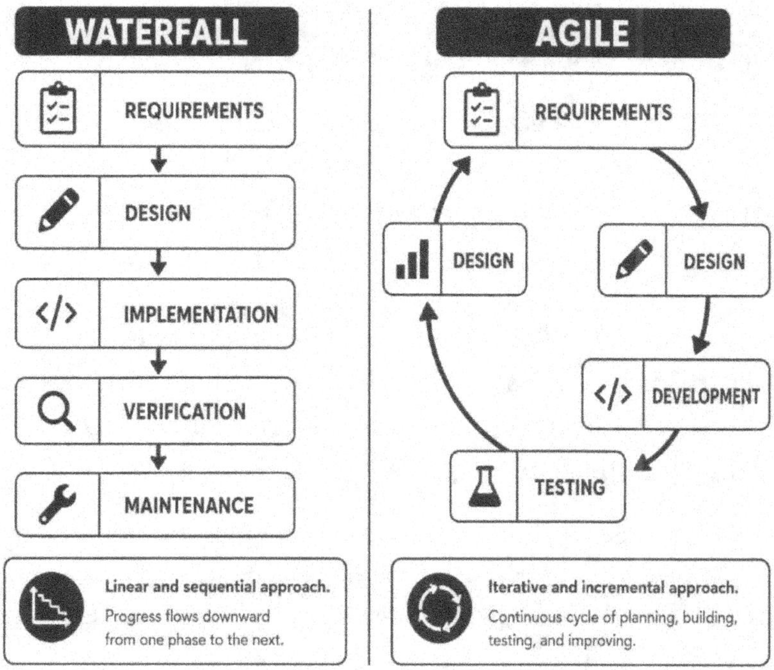

Methodologies in Practice

Waterfall: Structured Delivery

Imagine constructing a house strictly by blueprint. The architect's plan is finalized before the first brick is laid. Walls rise in sequence, plumbing and wiring follow, and finishing touches come last. The beauty of this approach is its clarity: everyone knows the plan, and progress is visible step by step.

This is Waterfall. It thrives in contexts where certainty is prized: bridges, skyscrapers, regulated systems. Each stage flows into the next, leaving little ambiguity. Yet the very strength of Waterfall is also its constraint; once walls are up, adjustments require careful planning.

AI may accelerate documentation, compliance activities, and simulation exercises, but the delivery model remains structured, with each stage completed before the next begins.

Agile: Adaptive Delivery

Now picture building a house room by room. The living room takes shape first, and feedback from its use informs how the kitchen is designed. The house evolves with its occupants, adapting to their changing needs.

This is Agile. It thrives in environments where responsiveness matters: startups, creative teams, evolving products. Like a restaurant kitchen, Agile adjusts dishes based on customer feedback, experimenting with flavours while keeping service flowing. The workflow is adaptive, responsive, and shaped by continuous feedback.

Feedback loops can be enriched through **AI**, variations suggested, repetitive prep automated, insights surfaced, but improvisation still demands discipline. Without a guiding vision, iterative delivery can become fragmented and difficult to align.

The Choreographed Blend: Hybrid

Many teams choose a blend. It is like film production: the script and budget are locked, but shooting and editing adapt to creative input. Structured where predictability is important, yet adaptive where learning and feedback add value.

This is Hybrid. It balances predictability with flexibility, offering the stability of Waterfall and the adaptability of Agile. Documentation may flow quickly through **AI**, while iterative coding gains support, creating a bridge between planning and adaptability.

Methodology shapes how teams organize work. Whether you choose Waterfall, Agile, or a hybrid approach, the process should reflect the needs, constraints, and goals of the project.

Beyond Software

In ***the Orchestra,*** musicians follow a defined score and sequence of rehearsals. Success depends on coordination, preparation, and adherence to a shared plan.

Improvisational theatre takes a different approach. Performers respond to changing situations in real time, adapting as new information emerges. This mirrors the flexibility often associated with Agile delivery.

Signals of Approach

These are not just labels; they are the signals that guide how teams move, adapt, and deliver. Each approach provides a framework for making decisions, coordinating work, and responding to change.

Foundations of the Cycle

- **SDLC**: The step-by-step journey software takes from idea to ongoing use.
- **Requirements**: The list of what the system must do before building starts.
- **Lifecycle Care**: Release and ongoing updates after launch.

Delivery Approaches

- **Waterfall**: A project style where everything is planned and built in sequence, like following a strict blueprint.
- **Agile**: A project style where work is done in small steps, adapting as feedback comes in.
- **Hybrid**: A mix of Waterfall's structure and Agile flexibility.

Iteration & Improvement

- **Methodology**: The way a team organizes work, collaboration, and delivery.
- **Iteration**: Repeating cycles of work to refine and improve.

These delivery choices may be invisible in the code itself, but they strongly influence how systems evolve, adapt, and endure over time.

Delivery Under Pressure

The project room was tense. A banking system upgrade had stalled because a single requirement was overlooked. In another corner of the industry, a startup was thriving by releasing features in quick bursts, adjusting to user feedback week by week. Two approaches, two outcomes: Waterfall and Agile.

Waterfall - The Traditional Blueprint

In Waterfall, requirements are locked up-front. Each stage must finish before the next begins, like following a strict blueprint. The process is orderly and predictable. Documentation, design diagrams, and test cases may be accelerated through **AI**, but foresight and compliance remain human craft. Developers focus on making requirements airtight, ensuring compliance, and anticipating risks before construction begins.

Agile - Building in Phases

Agile takes a different path. Work is divided into short sprints, each delivering usable increments. Delivery is iterative, shaped by feedback and collaboration. Sprint tasks, snippets, regression tests, and backlog grooming may be streamlined by **AI**, while collaboration and empathy stay human. Developers focus on facilitating teamwork, adapting to feedback, and aligning features with user needs as the product evolves.

Aspect	***Waterfall: The Traditional Blueprint***	***Agile: Building in Phases***
Process	Sequential stages, no overlap	Iterative sprints, continuous delivery

Flexibility	Low - changes are costly	High - feedback drives change
Best Fit	Banking systems, compliance-heavy apps	Startups, evolving products
AI Role	Documentation, design, testing	Sprint planning, code generation, regression testing
Developer Role	Risk management, compliance, foresight	Collaboration, adaptability, user empathy

Whether you follow a blueprint or deliver in iterations, the chosen methodology shapes the outcome. Waterfall offers predictability, Agile offers adaptability. **AI** may accelerate many activities, but successful delivery still depends on sound judgment, collaboration, and execution.

Think It Through

- In your own projects, where have you noticed **AI** making the biggest difference: in structured, blueprint-style work or in adaptive, sprint-based work?
- When you think about your current project, do you value clarity upfront or flexibility during development more? Why?
- If you had to explain the difference between Agile and Waterfall to a non-technical friend, how would you do it without jargon?

From Reflection to Action

Take a project idea, it could be something simple like planning a community event or designing a mobile app.

1. Write the requirements as if you were using **Waterfall**: everything finalized upfront, no changes allowed once building begins.
2. Rewrite the same idea as **Agile**: split it into 2–3 sprints, each delivering something usable, with feedback loops guiding the next step.
3. Compare the two versions: Where does **AI** help most? Where does human judgment matter most?

Having compared Waterfall and Agile, pause and reflect: the methodology shapes the process, but the mindset shapes the outcome. In the next section, we will explore the developer's mindset: how to balance ***AI's*** *assistance with critical thinking, and how to grow beyond prompts into real-world problem-solving.*

Case Study: Customer Support Chatbot

Over the past few years, a mid-sized e-commerce company receives thousands of customer inquiries each week related to order tracking, refunds, product issues, shipping updates, and account management. As the business grows, the support team faces increasing pressure to maintain fast response times while delivering a consistent customer experience.

Many requests are repetitive and require similar responses, leaving support agents with less time to focus on complex issues. During peak shopping periods, response queues grow longer, impacting both customer satisfaction and operational efficiency.

To address these challenges, the company decides to develop a Customer Support Chatbot capable of handling common customer interactions, providing self-service assistance, and escalating complex cases to human agents when necessary. The chatbot must also integrate with existing business systems, including customer databases, order management platforms, and support ticketing tools.

While the primary goal is to improve support efficiency, the solution must also be secure, scalable, maintainable, and resilient. Applying systems thinking throughout the Software Development Life Cycle (SDLC) helps ensure these considerations are addressed from planning through deployment and continuous improvement.

The following roadmap illustrates how systems thinking principles can be incorporated across each phase of the SDLC when building the Customer Support Chatbot.

SDLC for Customer Support Chatbot

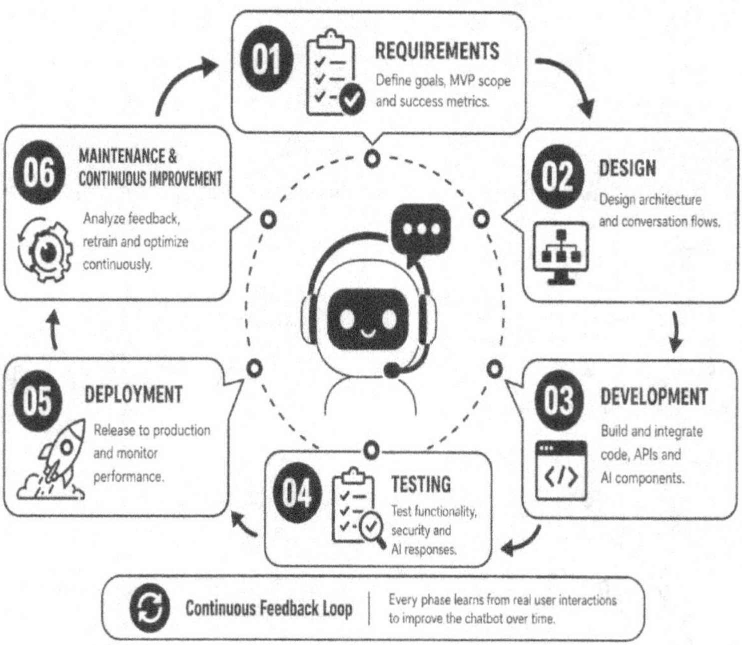

Requirements Phase

The journey begins with clarity. Before any dialog flows or architecture diagrams are drawn, the team must decide what the chatbot should achieve in its first release. This is where the MVP definition anchors the work:

MVP Scope: Handle order tracking and refund requests; escalate unresolved cases to human agents.

Backlog items may be drafted quickly through **AI**, then refined by analysts for completeness, security, and role-based access. A simple prompt: *"Generate Epics and User Stories for a customer support chatbot MVP with acceptance criteria"* produces a first draft.

The Business Analyst (BA) steps in to challenge the draft. By re-prompting **AI** for negative scenarios and role-based permissions, the BA ensures escalation rules, privacy checks, and security boundaries are embedded. This iterative cycle transforms raw output into responsible requirements.

Final Refined Story:

- *Epic:* Order Tracking
- *Story:* As a customer, I want to enter my order ID so I can track my delivery status.
- *Acceptance Criteria:*
  - If order ID is valid and belongs to logged-in user → chatbot retrieves delivery status.
  - If order ID is invalid → chatbot prompts for re-entry or escalates.
  - If order ID belongs to another user → chatbot denies access and escalates.

The Requirements Phase is not just about listing features; it is about framing the system responsibly. **AI** accelerates drafting, but human judgment ensures requirements are secure, role-aware, and testable. This collaboration produces backlog items that are both fast to generate and robust enough for implementation.

Design Phase

With requirements clarified and validated, the team now turns to **designing the chatbot's architecture and conversation flows**. This is the creative stage where ideas are sketched, debated, and refined. The goal is to translate Epics and Stories into a **high-level system design** that shows how the chatbot will interact with users, backend systems, and support agents. Brainstorming sessions set the tone:

- ➢ What should the user's first experience with the chatbot feel like?
- ➢ How do we ensure conversations are natural, yet structured enough to guide users?
- ➢ Where do we place guardrails for errors, escalations, and permissions?
- ➢ How do backend systems (order database, refund API, ticketing system) connect seamlessly?

Sticky notes and whiteboards capture user journeys, while team debates anchor the design in empathy. Dialog variations may be scaffolded by **AI**, but designers embed tone, escalation rules, and security boundaries to keep flows intuitive and responsible.

From brainstorming, the team distils a **high-level architecture** that captures the system's moving parts:

1. User Interface Layer
   – Web widget, mobile app integration, and optional messaging channels.

2. Conversation Layer (NLP + Dialog Manager)
   – Intent recognition (e.g., "Track Order")
   – Entity extraction (e.g., Order ID)
   – Dialog flow management (guiding user through steps)
3. Business Logic Layer
   – Order Tracking Service → queries order database
   – Refund Service → triggers refund API
   – Escalation Service → creates ticket and connects to agent
4. Data & Security Layer
   – Authentication → ensures logged-in user context
   – Role-based access → prevents cross-user data leaks
   – Logging & monitoring → tracks queries and escalations
5. Human Agent Integration
   – Ticketing system → integrates with existing support workflows
   – Escalation triggers → connect the user to a human agent when confidence is low

Example Dialog Flow (Track My Order)

Flow Steps:

1. Greeting and Request - The chatbot greets the user and asks for the order ID.
   – Bot: "Hello! How can I help you today?"
   – User: "Where's my order?"
   – Bot: "Sure, can you share your order ID?"
   – User: "12345"

2. Authentication & Validation - The system checks if the order belongs to the logged-in user.
   – If valid → proceed
   – If invalid → prompt re-entry or escalate

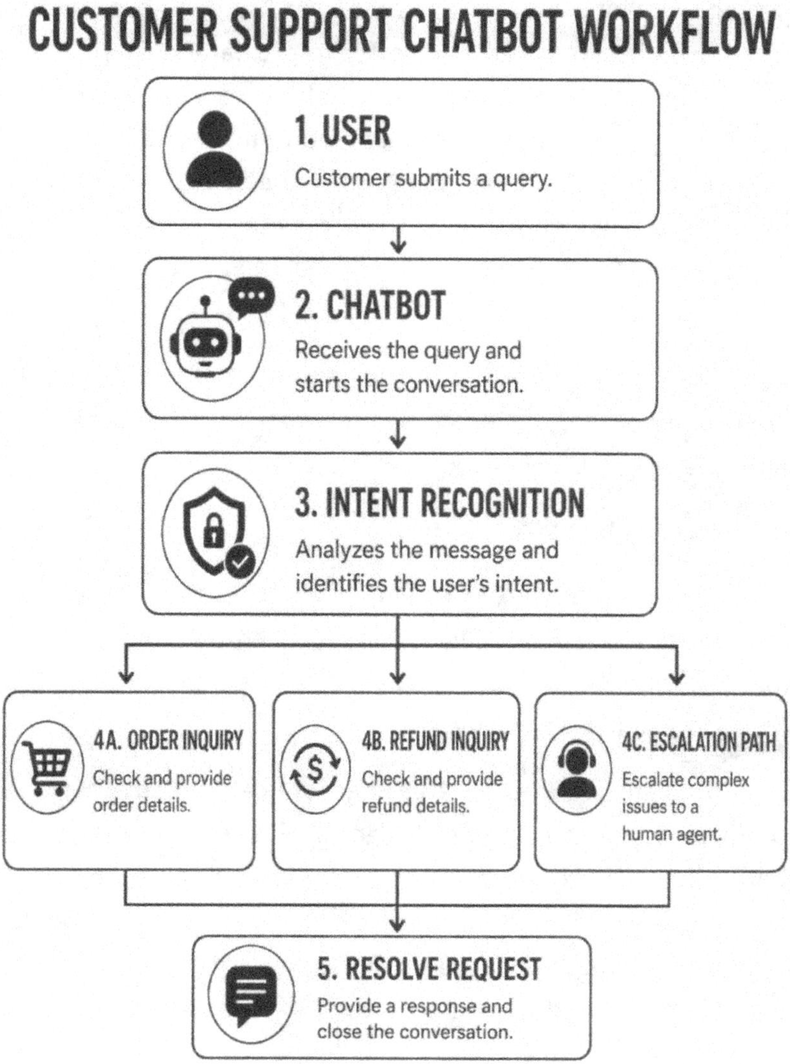

3. Positive Path - If valid, the chatbot retrieves and displays the delivery status.
   – Bot: "Your order is out for delivery and should arrive by Tuesday."
4. Negative Path (Invalid ID/ Cross-user Access) - The chatbot prompts for re-entry or offer to escalate.
   – Bot: "That order ID does not look right. Please try again or I can connect you to an agent."
5. Escalation - In both negative cases, the chatbot creates a ticket and connects the user to a human agent.
   – Bot: "I will create a support ticket and connect you to a human agent."

This flow mirrors the requirements acceptance criteria we refined earlier, including positive path, invalid ID handling, and role-based access enforcement.

Business Analyst's Role in Design

The BA ensures design flows remain faithful to requirements by validating dialog paths, embedding escalation logic, confirming role-based access, and collaborating with UX designers to keep flows accessible.

Design is where the chatbot begins to feel real. Brainstorming immerses the team in the customer's journey, while architecture diagrams ensure resilience and security. By blending creativity with structure and balancing **AI** scaffolding with human judgment, the team creates a design that is both user-centred and system-ready, setting the stage for development.

Development Phase

Requirements and design established the rules, flows, and architectural boundaries. Development is where those ideas become operational software. The MVP focuses on three primary intents: order tracking, refund requests, and escalation handling. From there, the team delivers incrementally, embedding qualities such as integration, security, operational stability, extensibility, and monitoring into each sprint.

AI assists with dialog scaffolding, artifact generation, and personalization workflows, but engineering accountability remains with the development team. Generated outputs still require architectural review, security validation, and operational testing before release.

Agile Sprints in Practice

Development progresses through focused sprints; each tied directly to requirements and design decisions:

Sprint	*Goals*	*System Attribute Focus*
Sprint 1	Order tracking with authentication and database query.	Integration + Security
Sprint 2	Refund flow with API integration and failure handling.	Resilience + Monitoring

Sprint 3	Escalation flow with ticketing system and fallback logic.	Coordination + Recovery
Sprint 4	Logging, monitoring, and analytics instrumentation.	Observability + Maintainability
Sprint 5	UX refinement, personalization, and pilot rollout.	Scalability + Maintainability

This delivery cadence transforms conceptual models into deployable capabilities while reinforcing the operational characteristics expected from production systems.

Systems Thinking

Every implementation decision reflects systems-thinking principles, helping the team understand not only how the chatbot works, but how it behaves within a larger operational environment:

- **Purpose**: Reduce support workload while improving customer experience; Automation handles repetitive scaffolding so developers can focus on architecture and edge conditions.
- **Interactions**: APIs, NLP services, databases, and escalation workflows must operate as a connected ecosystem rather than isolated components.

  chatbot ↔ NLP ↔ services ↔ databases
- **Boundaries**: Authentication, authorization, and compliance controls ensure users access only their own data.

➢ **Perspectives**: The solution must support multiple stakeholders, including customers, support agents, operations teams, and business owners.
➢ **Feedback**: Logs, test outcomes, escalation metrics, and API failures guide refinement across sprints.
➢ **Time**: Prompts, workflows, and operational practices evolve continuously as the product matures.

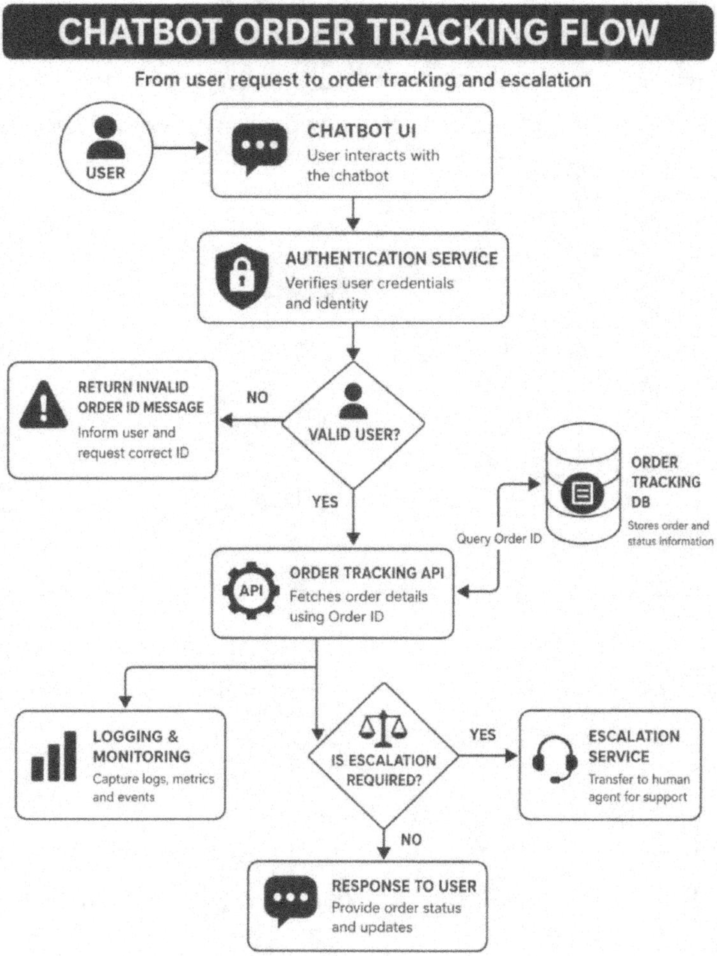

AI Prompts

AI-generated scripts and templates accelerate implementation, but generated artifacts still require engineering review for compliance, reliability, and operational readiness.

For Example: Database Script Creation

Prompt: "Generate a SQL script to create an Orders table with fields for order id, user id, product name, status, and created timestamp. Include constraints for primary key and foreign key linking to User Table".

```
Output: CREATE TABLE Orders (
  order_id INT PRIMARY KEY,
  user_id INT NOT NULL,
  product_name VARCHAR (255),
  status VARCHAR (50),
  created_at TIMESTAMP DEFAULT
CURRENT_TIMESTAMP,
 FOREIGN KEY (user_id) REFERENCES
Users(user_id)
);
```

In practice, production databases may also require indexing, auditing fields, retention policies, and additional security controls beyond the generated draft.

APIs, logging formats, validation rules, and operational checklists follow a similar pattern: automation accelerates drafting, while developers validate correctness, security, and maintainability.

Acceptance-Test Matrix

Acceptance criteria flow directly into validation activities, ensuring requirements translate into measurable and repeatable outcomes. For example:

User Story	***Acceptance Criteria***	***Test Case***	***Expected Result***
Track Order	Order must belong to logged-in user	Enter valid order ID	Accurate status in natural language
Track Order	Invalid ID rejected	Enter random ID	Error + escalation option
Refund Request	Refund API triggered	Submit valid refund request	Refund initiated
Escalation	Low NLP confidence escalates	Enter ambiguous query	Ticket created + agent connected

This traceability between requirements, implementation, and testing keeps chatbot behaviour predictable, auditable, and reliable.

Operational Readiness

As the chatbot matures, the focus shifts from feature delivery to reliable operations and continuous monitoring:

- **KPIs & SLAs**
  - – NLP intent accuracy ≥ 90%
  - – API latency ≤ 500ms
  - – Escalation rate monitored at ≤ 15%
  - – Error budget defined per sprint
- **Rollout Strategy**
  - – Feature flags for controlled releases
  - – Canary deployments before full rollout
  - – Monitoring and rollback plans in place
- **Runbooks (Examples)**
  - – Document procedures for service failures, outages, and model degradation
  - – Define escalation paths and recovery actions
  - – **Refund API Timeout**: Retry → Escalate → Alert DevOps
  - – **Database Outage**: Switch to read replica → Alert DBA
  - – **NLP Drift**: Retrain model → Validate accuracy → Redeploy
- **Security Checklist**
  - – Secure authentication and token management
  - – Encryption at rest and in transit
  - – **PII** (Personally Identifiable Information) protection and access control
  - – Role-based access verified in every service call

Continuous Feedback

Every sprint ends with a **feedback loop**:

- **AI-generated prompts** are reviewed, refined, and tested.
- **Logs** highlight which variations improve NLP accuracy.
- **Quality engineer validation** ensures outputs align with requirements and guardrails.
- **Developers adjust prompts** for the next sprint, embedding lessons learned.

This loop ensures the system is not static: it learns, adapts, and evolves with each iteration.

By the end of development, the chatbot is more than a functional feature set. It becomes an operational platform designed for reliability, visibility, security, extensibility, and controlled growth. Each sprint reinforces the connection between requirements, architecture, testing, and deployment, demonstrating that software delivery is a continuous and interconnected system rather than a sequence of isolated phases.

Testing Phase

Testing is woven into every sprint, moving alongside development rather than following it. Developers and Quality Assurance (QA) engineers collaborate from the outset, sharing scenarios, acceptance criteria, and test strategies during sprint planning. This approach ensures that unit and component testing are addressed during implementation, while QA focuses on validating behaviour across integrated services and production-like environments.

Coordinated Workflow

- During Development
    - Developers create unit tests for functions, APIs, and dialog flows.
    - Component tests verify interactions between modules such as authentication and order tracking.
    - **AI** generated test cases can expand coverage, while engineers review them for relevance, completeness, and risk.
- During QA Integration Testing
    - QA engineers validate end-to-end journeys across connected services.
    - Integration tests confirm that APIs, databases, NLP services, and escalation workflows operate correctly together.
    - Performance, security, and monitoring capabilities are evaluated from a system perspective.

For Example: Test Case Collaboration

During Sprint 2 (Refund Flow), developers and QA engineers align on shared validation scenarios:

- **Unit Test:** Confirm the refund API returns success for valid inputs.
- **Component Test:** Verify the refund service interacts correctly with authentication and database services.

- **Integration Test:** Simulate the complete journey from chatbot UI → authentication → NLP → refund API → logging.

This layered strategy provides confidence at multiple levels while reducing duplicated effort.

AI Prompts

AI can accelerate test preparation by generating cases, edge scenarios, and draft scripts:

- **Unit Tests:** "Write Python unit tests for the order tracking API covering valid orders, invalid orders, and unauthorized access."
- **Edge Scenarios:** "Suggest five edge cases for refund requests that could expose failures or unexpected behaviour."
- **Integration Testing:** "Generate a test script that simulates a user tracking an order through the chatbot UI, authentication, NLP, API, and database layers."
- **Monitoring Thresholds:** "Propose alert thresholds for escalation rates and API latency during integration testing."

Generated artifacts provide a starting point, but engineers remain responsible for validating assumptions, refining scenarios, and ensuring coverage aligns with business requirements.

Validating System Qualities

Testing verifies the operational qualities introduced during development:

- **Integration:** Confirm services exchange data correctly and consistently.
- **Scalability:** Use load testing to evaluate behaviour under peak demand.
- **Reliability:** Introduce failures to validate retry logic, fallback paths, and recovery mechanisms.
- **Security:** Verify authentication controls, encryption, and access restrictions.
- **Maintainability:** Run regression suites to ensure new capabilities do not disrupt existing behaviour.
- **Observability:** Confirm logs, dashboards, and alerts provide meaningful operational insight.

Feedback into Delivery

Testing continuously informs future development activities:

- Failed unit or component tests trigger immediate corrections within the sprint.
- Integration findings highlight architectural or workflow improvements.
- Monitoring results expose bottlenecks, failure patterns, and operational risks.
- New scenarios discovered during testing expand future coverage.

Rather than acting as a gate at the end of delivery, testing becomes an ongoing source of learning. Each cycle improves confidence in the chatbot's behaviour, helping teams identify weaknesses before they affect customers.

The Testing Phase demonstrates that software quality is built throughout delivery, not inspected in at the end. Developers establish confidence through unit and component testing, while QA engineers validate behaviour across integrated systems. Together, they ensure the chatbot performs reliably under real-world conditions and remains ready for production use.

Deployment & Monitoring Phase

Deployment unfolds through staged releases and continuous evaluation rather than a single high-risk launch. The team introduces the chatbot incrementally, using rollout strategies that reduce operational risk while gathering real-world insights:

- **Feature Flags**: Enable or disable specific intents (e.g., refund flow) for subsets of users.
- **Canary Release**: Roll out to 10% of users first, monitor performance, then expand.
- **Rollback Plan**: Maintain versioned deployments so the system can revert quickly if needed.

Monitoring in Real Time

Once deployed, monitoring becomes the heartbeat of the system. Developers and QA engineers collaborate to track:

- **Performance Metrics**: API latency, NLP accuracy, escalation rates.
- **Resilience Signals**: Retry counts, fallback triggers, circuit breaker activations.
- **Security Alerts**: Unauthorized access attempts, token misuse, encryption failures.
- **User Experience**: Satisfaction scores, feedback ratings, abandonment rates.

Dashboards and alerts notify the team when thresholds are breached, enabling rapid response. **AI-driven anomaly detection** further accelerates issue identification.

Systems Thinking

Production deployment offers the first opportunity to observe how the system behaves under real customer demand. The six lenses of systems thinking help teams interpret those signals:

- **Purpose**: Ensure the chatbot delivers consistent value in production.
- **Interactions**: Monitor how services interact under real load.
- **Boundaries**: Control rollout scope with feature flags and canaries.
- **Perspectives**: Balance customer experience, agent workload, and business KPIs.
- **Feedback**: Use monitoring data and user ratings to refine prompts and flows.

- **Time**: Plan for continuous updates, retraining, and scaling over time.

Continuous Learning

Production data becomes a valuable source of insight:

- Monitoring trends influence future development priorities.
- Customer feedback highlights opportunities to improve dialog flows and user experience.
- Operational incidents reveal areas where reliability or recovery mechanisms can be strengthened.
- **AI**-generated summaries help teams identify recurring themes across support tickets, alerts, and retrospectives.

These insights ensure that decisions are guided by real usage patterns rather than assumptions made during development.

Launch marks the beginning of operational learning rather than the completion of delivery. By combining monitoring, customer feedback, and production metrics, teams gain a clearer understanding of how the chatbot performs in the real world. Those insights guide future improvements, helping the solution remain aligned with user expectations and business objectives.

Maintenance & Continuous Improvement Phase

Maintenance begins once the chatbot is operating in production. The focus shifts from feature delivery to sustaining performance, addressing emerging issues, and incorporating lessons learned from monitoring, customer feedback, and QA validation. Regular updates, model retraining, and workflow refinements help the solution remain effective as business needs change.

Team Collaboration Beyond Release

- **Production Support:** Teams work together to maintain reliability, address issues, and improve the chatbot experience.
- **Developers**: Address issues flagged in logs, refine dialog flows, and update prompts.
- **QA Engineers**: Validate fixes, run regression tests, and confirm that new features do not break existing ones.
- **Shared Ownership**: Both teams review monitoring dashboards together, ensuring alignment on priorities.

AI Prompts

Maintenance relies on collaboration across engineering and quality teams. **AI** can assist by generating regression suites, suggesting monitoring enhancements, and drafting retrospective summaries, while teams remain responsible for validating outputs and prioritizing changes.

- **Generate Regression Test Suites:** "Create regression test cases for order tracking and refund flows after a new escalation feature is added."
- **Suggest Monitoring Enhancements:** "Propose new metrics to track chatbot personalization effectiveness."

- **Draft Retrospective Summaries:** "Summarize sprint feedback into key improvement themes for the next cycle."
- **Policy Updates:** "Write a checklist for updating chatbot security policies after a new compliance requirement."

Systems Thinking

Maintenance reflects the same six conceptual lenses:

- **Purpose**: Keep the chatbot aligned with business goals and user needs.
- **Interactions**: Monitor evolving integrations (new APIs, updated databases).
- **Boundaries**: Ensure updates do not expand scope beyond intended use.
- **Perspectives**: Balance customer satisfaction, agent workload, and compliance.
- **Feedback**: Use monitoring data, user ratings, and QA reports to guide improvements.
- **Time**: Plan for retraining cycles, version upgrades, and long-term scalability.

Improvement Cycle

Operational data, customer feedback, and testing outcomes continue to shape future work:

- **Monitoring → Development**: Logs and metrics highlight weak points.
- **User Feedback → Design**: Comments and ratings inform dialog refinements.

- **QA → Testing**: Regression failures guide new test cases.
- **AI Prompts → Efficiency**: Generate artifacts faster, freeing developers to focus on architecture.

The Maintenance & Continuous Improvement Phase ensures that the chatbot remains effective long after release. Through ongoing collaboration, operational review, and targeted enhancements, teams preserve service quality while adapting to changing customer expectations, business priorities, and technical requirements.

This case study illustrates that successful chatbot delivery requires more than implementing features. Every phase, from requirements through maintenance, contributes to qualities such as ***security, reliability, observability, extensibility, and operational readiness***. These characteristics emerge through deliberate design decisions rather than being added at the end.

The lifecycle also demonstrates how each phase informs the next. Requirements influence design, design shapes implementation, testing validates behaviour, and production insights guide future enhancements. Monitoring data, customer feedback, and retrospective findings become inputs for subsequent iterations, creating a continuous cycle of improvement.

Generative AI contributes throughout this journey by accelerating research, drafting artifacts, expanding test coverage, and supporting operational analysis. However, responsibility for architecture, governance, security, and quality remains with the people building and operating the system.

Ultimately, the value of **systems thinking** lies in helping teams see beyond individual tasks and consider how decisions affect the broader ecosystem. By combining human judgment with **AI-assisted** delivery, organizations can build solutions that remain **robust**, **adaptable**, and **sustainable** long after their initial release.

Closing Thoughts

You have seen how the Software Development Life Cycle (SDLC) provides the rhythm behind every feature. Each stage, requirements, design, development, testing, deployment, and maintenance, acts as a checkpoint that keeps the system strong.

- **Requirements:** clarify user needs before code begins.
- **Design**: plan for scalability, security, and compliance.
- **Development:** cover edge cases and write maintainable logic.
- **Testing**: validate functionality and anticipate risks.
- **Deployment:** ensure observability and rollback plans.
- **Maintenance**: adapt to evolving dependencies.

Carry this mindset*: treat the SDLC as your blueprint, a choreography where phases move in sync, whether in linear Waterfall or iterative Agile.* ***AI*** *can accelerate tasks at every stage, but it is your judgment that ensures features fit into the bigger picture.*

In Part III, you will see how this process connects to real-world readiness, with habits like resilience, collaboration, and debugging that transform systems from functional prototypes into production-ready solutions.

Part III
Real World Readiness

Chapter 5: Thinking Beyond Code

When Code Is Not Enough

It is late evening in a bustling co-working space. Screens glow with lines of code, and a developer leans back, satisfied that the login flow compiles without errors. The syntax is clean, the functions run, and the **AI** assistant generated half the scaffolding in seconds. On the surface, it looks like progress.

But then the questions begin: *What happens if ten thousand users log in at once? What if the database slows down?* What if someone tries to break in? The code may be correct, but correctness is only the first step. True readiness comes from seeing beyond syntax, imagining how this piece of logic interacts with APIs, databases, networks, and people.

Earlier, we explored systems thinking through engineering attributes such as scalability, resilience, and security. Here, those attributes return in practice, shaping how correct code becomes truly production-ready.

Generative **AI** can assemble flows in seconds, but the craft of a developer lies in designing for systems that endure under stress, scale with demand, and remain secure against threats.

AI can suggest architectures, safeguards, and implementation patterns, but deciding which trade-offs are appropriate for a specific system remains a human responsibility. Writing code is only the beginning; **systems thinking** is what makes it usable in the real world.

When you write, think beyond syntax. Consider:

- **Integration patterns**: how components talk to each other?
- **Scalability**: can the system grow without breaking?
- **Resilience**: how does it bounce back if something fails?
- **Application security**: how do you keep intruders out?
- **Performance**: does it still run smoothly under load?
- **Observability**: can you see problems before users do?
- **Maintainability**: can future developers extend it easily?
- **Documentation**: does the story of your system live on?

From Structure to Sustainability

Imagine you have built a house with **AI**-powered robots that can instantly install furniture and wiring. That is coding today: fast, efficient, and impressive at first glance. But unless you have thought about scalability, resilience, security, and maintainability, the house may look fine yet fail when everyone tries to live in it at once.

At first, one family fits comfortably. But when ten families move in, the plumbing clogs, the power grid strains, and the rooms feel overcrowded. The structure does not collapse, but the experience becomes unsustainable. Then a storm hits: drainage, backup power, and reinforced walls decide whether the house remains liveable. Stylish doors and windows may look modern, but without locks, intruders walk right in. Furniture is installed, yet if it cannot be rearranged without tearing down walls, every change becomes demolition. And without blueprints, future builders will not know where the wiring runs or how the foundation was laid.

Secure and Resilient Login Flow

Just as a house must withstand storms and intruders, a login flow must endure failures and attacks. From browser to database, each step in the login process must be designed with resilience and security in mind. Below is a **visual flow diagram** that captures those checkpoints:

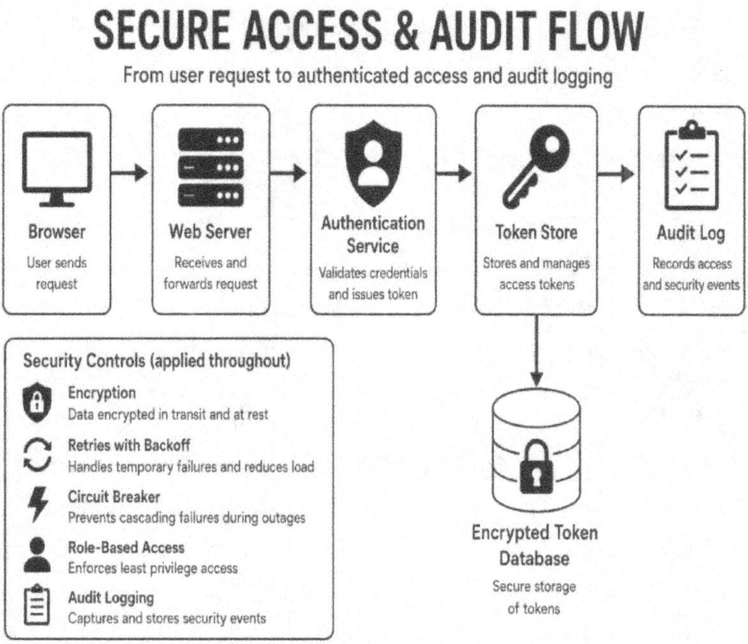

The login flow may seem like a technical example, but the same principles apply to payment systems, chatbots, dashboards, booking platforms, and countless other systems. Every system, whether digital or physical, succeeds or fails based on its ability to handle real-world complexity.

Beyond Software

A **hospital** gleams with new machines, each capable of miracles, yet when an emergency strikes, chaos unfolds because protocols were not rehearsed, staff were not trained, and patient data security was an afterthought.

Across town, a **city** celebrates its freshly paved roads. The ribbon is cut, traffic surges, and within weeks, the lanes choke with congestion. Maintenance schedules lag, safety checks slip, and the system built for speed begins to crumble under its own momentum.

In a **school**, tablets arrive overnight. Students tap eagerly, but lessons stall because the curriculum has not adapted, teachers have not been trained, and accessibility remains an afterthought.

Whether it is hospitals, highways, or classrooms, the pattern repeats***: speed of construction is not the same as readiness for real use***. Systems thinking is what turns structures into sustainable ecosystems, the difference between something that merely works and something that endures.

Invisible Architecture

These are not just technical terms; they are the hidden structures that keep systems alive under pressure. Each one is a safeguard, a signal, or a promise that your design will hold when reality pushes back.

Resilience Patterns

- **Timeouts:** Defines how long a request waits before failing, preventing resource exhaustion.
- **Retries with Backoff:** Spaces out repeated attempts to avoid overwhelming services.
- **Circuit Breaker:** Stops requests to failing services to prevent cascading failures.
- **Fallback Provider:** A secondary service (e.g., email provider) used when the primary fails, ensuring continuity.
- **Caching:** Stores frequently accessed data closer to users, reducing database load and improving response times during peak demand.

Security Foundations

- **Encryption in Transit:** Secures data as it moves between components, protecting credentials.
- **Role Checks:** Verifies user permissions to enforce least-privilege access.
- **Audit Trail:** Captures every security event for compliance and monitoring.

Operational Readiness

- **Incident Playbook**: A structured response plan: Detect → Isolate → Mitigate → Learn.
- **Runbook**: A documented set of steps for handling incidents, rollbacks, and postmortems.
- **SLO (Service Level Objective)**: A target measure of reliability or performance agreed upon by the team.

Performance Signals

- **p95 Latency:** Shows how quickly 95% of requests complete, highlighting slow "tail" requests.
- **Token Failures**: Errors in authentication token generation or validation that block successful logins.
- **Queue Depth**: Measures how many requests are waiting in a queue, often an early sign of overload.

Together, these terms form the invisible architecture of reliability, the quiet design choices that make systems trustworthy.

Signals in Motion

Metrics are not just numbers on a dashboard; they are the pulse of your system. Each one tells a story about what is happening behind the scenes. When latency spikes, it is the system gasping for breath. When error rates climb, it is users hitting locked doors. When queue depth grows, it is traffic piling up at a bottleneck. The table below is not just thresholds; it is a set of early warning signals that help you catch trouble before it becomes an incident.

Try this: As you read each metric, imagine the real-world user experience it represents. What does a 500 *ms* delay feel like when you are logging in? What happens when password reset emails do not arrive?

Metric	Why it matters	Alert rule (example)
p95 latency	Catches tail latency that impacts real users	p95 > 500 *ms* for 5m
Error rate	Shows functional failures blocking users	error rate > 1% for 5m
Token failures	Directly prevents successful logins	token failures > 0.5% for 5m
Email delivery	Critical for reset flows and recovery	delivery success < 95% for 10m
Queue depth	Early sign of downstream overload	queue depth > baseline + 3σ

Metrics are not abstract; they are signals that tell a story. Listen before they become screams.

Flashlight in the Dark

Incidents rarely announce themselves politely. They arrive as alerts, spikes, or angry user reports. The playbook below is not just a checklist; it is a survival guide. Think of it as the flashlight you grab when the lights go out. Step by step flow (with prompts):

- **Detect**: When an alert fires, check p95 latency (how fast 95% of requests finish), error rate, token failures, and email delivery.
  Try this: imagine you are the on-call engineer at 2 a.m. Which metric would you check first, and why?
- **Isolate**: Correlate anomalies with recent deploys or specific regions. Narrow the blast radius before panic spreads.
- **Mitigate**:
  – If the database is slow → enable a cached path or temporarily increase the database pool.
  – If the email provider fails → switch to a fallback or show a clear user message.
  – If the token store is overloaded → throttle non-critical requests.
  Brainstorm: which of these mitigations would you automate, and which require human judgment?
- **Learn**: After mitigation, run smoke tests, document the root cause, and update the runbook. Every incident is tuition; the lesson is resilience.

Every incident is a rehearsal for the next one. The faster you move from chaos to clarity, the stronger your system becomes.

Backstage Ritual

Shipping code is like opening night at the theatre. The rehearsals are over, the lights are on, and the audience is waiting. But before the curtain rises, every detail must be checked: the sound system, the exits, the costumes. In software, production readiness is that backstage ritual. It is the difference between a smooth premiere and chaos in front of your users.

Checklist

- **Observability**: Metrics are your spotlight. p95 latency, error rate, token failures, email delivery, and queue depth each one tells you if the system is performing or faltering.
  Try this: imagine you are on-call and one of these metrics' spikes. Which one would you trust first to guide your response?
- **Resilience**: Timeouts, retries with backoff, circuit breakers, fallback email providers. These are your safety nets. They do not stop the fall, but they make sure you land without breaking.
  Brainstorm: which of these safeguards would you automate, and which would you keep manual for control?
- **Security**: TLS in transit, encryption at rest, role checks, least privilege. Locks on every door, keys only for those who need them.
  Pause: if you had to explain "least privilege" to a non-technical teammate, how would you do it?
- **Testing**: Smoke tests, one test account per role, basic load test for p95. Dress rehearsals before opening night.
  Try this: what is the smallest test you could run that would still give you confidence before a big launch?

- **Runbooks**: Short incident playbook, rollback steps, postmortem owner. Scripts for when things go wrong, so panic does not take over.
- **Docs**: API contracts, SLOs, monitoring dashboard links in pull request. The blueprint that ensures future builders know where the wiring runs.

Preparation is the quiet work that makes confidence possible. Production readiness is not about perfection; it is about preparation. The checklist is your ritual, your way of saying: we are ready for whatever the audience throws at us. Readiness is resilience rehearsed, the quiet discipline that makes trust visible.

Think It Through

- When you generate code with **AI**, do you pause to ask: *How will this behave under stress or failure?*
- In your current project, how do you balance speed of delivery with long-term resilience?
- Imagine a login flow under heavy load. What cracks appear first, and which safeguards would you add?
- How does your team ensure the system's story lives on for future developers through documentation?
- Think back to your last incident. Was it treated as a nuisance or as an opportunity to learn? What would you change in hindsight?

From Reflection to Action

Take a simple coding task (e.g., building a login flow).

1. Use **AI** to generate the basic code.
2. Now, sketch a low-level design:
   - How will the login interact with the database?
   - What APIs are involved?
   - How will performance scale if 10,000 users log in at once?
   - What resilience measures exist if the database crashes?
   - What security checks prevent unauthorized access?
   - How will future developers maintain or extend this flow?

Compare: Did the ***AI****-generated code alone solves the problem, or did your system-level design make it truly usable in the real world?*

Systems are more than syntax. They are houses built to be lived in, not just admired. **AI** accelerates the build, but it is **your systems thinking** that ensures the structure stands strong.

"But systems are not built alone. Next, we will see how collaboration becomes the cement that holds everything together."

Chapter 6: Building Together

Collaboration as the Foundation

The login flow is live, dashboards glow green, and the playbooks are rehearsed. On the surface, everything looks ready. But backstage, cracks form if the people around the system do not move in sync. Collaboration is the invisible force that keeps everything standing. Without it, even the cleanest code becomes brittle.

Generative AI can help you write code faster, but speed alone does not build a system that lasts. Think of a house: bricklayers raise walls, plumbers run pipes, electricians wire outlets. If they work in isolation, the walls stand but the water has nowhere to flow, and the lights never turn on.

Software systems are no different. Architects design the structure, developers lay the foundation, DevOps ensures smooth wiring across environments, and security specialists check every lock. Each role matters, but only collaboration ensures the structure holds together.

As a developer, your code is just one brick in the wall. Collaboration means seeing how your brick connects to others, how communication prevents cracks, and how shared effort ensures the house stands strong.

Cracks in the Blueprint

The house is almost ready. After months of work, the walls are painted, the wiring is hidden behind finished surfaces, and the plumbing has been installed. From the street, everything looks complete.

During the final walkthrough, a problem appears. The electrician pauses in front of a wall and realizes a required cable was never installed. The wall must now be opened again. Moments later, the plumber points out that a newly added fixture conflicts with an existing pipe. As the team retraces their steps, another issue emerges: a design change approved weeks earlier never reached everyone working on the project.

The delay is frustrating because nobody was careless. The electrician followed the plan. The plumber completed the installation correctly. The builders finished their work on schedule.

The problem was not effort or skill. The problem was communication.

Software projects often experience the same challenge. A developer builds a feature based on one set of requirements. A product manager updates the expectation. QA tests the original behaviour. DevOps prepares deployment while the operations team prepares monitoring and runbook based on outdated assumptions.

Each person does their job well. Yet when information fails to move between teams, small gaps become larger problems. The issue rarely begins with bad intentions; it begins when assumptions replace conversations.

Collaboration is not simply working alongside other people. It is ensuring that information, decisions, and expectations move as reliably as the code itself.

Think about your last project: which "role" did you rely on most, and what happened when communication slipped?

Beyond Software

Collaboration is the foundation of every complex system, not just software.

On a **film** set, the director calls *"action,"* but the sound engineer misses the cue. The scene looks perfect on camera, yet the final cut feels broken.

On the **field**, a striker delivers a flawless pass, but the teammate is not ready. The ball rolls away, and trust breaks with it.

In an **emergency**, sirens wail as firefighters arrive, but medics are delayed. What could have been contained turns into chaos.

Pause and reflect: which of these stories mirrors your own team? Where have you seen collaboration hold the line, and where did silence let cracks appear?

The Language of Collaboration

These are not just definitions; they are the shorthand teams use when systems are under stress. Each term is a thread in the fabric of teamwork, invisible until the moment it is needed.

Foundations

- **Cross-functional collaboration**: Different roles (developers, QA, DevOps, product, security) working together toward shared outcomes.
- **Shared ownership**: The mindset that resilience and success belong to the whole team, not just one role.
- **Alignment**: Ensuring technical priorities and business goals move in the same direction.

Flows

- **Communication loops**: Structured feedback channels that prevent silos and ensure information flows both ways.
- **Knowledge transfer**: Sharing context and insights so teammates can act without guesswork. Without knowledge sharing, teams create silos where critical context exists in only one person's head.

Safety Nets

- **Psychological safety**: A team environment where people feel safe to admit mistakes, ask questions, and learn openly.
- **Incident drills**: Practice runs that test not just systems but how teams coordinate under pressure.

Together, these terms form the language of collaboration: the invisible threads that hold systems and teams alike.

When Silence Breaks Systems

You are working on a new checkout flow for an e-commerce site. The deadline is tight, and **AI** can generate the payment code in seconds. It is tempting to stop there: the code works, the tests pass, and the feature look ready. But launch day tells a different story.

The first customers click **"Buy Now"**. The Frontend shows "***Payment Successful"***, but the backend rejects half the transactions. Refund requests pile up, but QA never flagged the edge cases. Support tickets flood in, and DevOps scrambles because monitoring was not set up to catch the spike. Meanwhile, the product owner discovers compliance requirements were missed, and the feature cannot legally stay online.

What looked polished in isolation collapses under pressure. The checkout flow becomes a bottleneck, the team scrambles to patch gaps, and trust with customers erodes. All because collaboration was skipped.

Snippet thinking: prompting **AI**, generate the payment code, and move on.**AI** can generate individual pieces of the solution, but only collaboration connects those pieces into a system that works in practice.

Systems thinking with collaboration:

➢ Align with the product owner on business requirement, customer expectation and release priorities.

- ➢ Sync with the frontend team to ensure the UI matches backend logic.
- ➢ Talk to QA to understand edge cases (failed payments, refunds).
- ➢ Review the payment flow with security teams to validate authentication, authorization, and protection of sensitive customer data.
- ➢ Check with DevOps about deployment pipelines, monitoring, and rollback plans.

Each of these conversations uncovers risks that are easy to miss when viewed from a single role. The table below shows how different team members contribute to the checkout flow and what can happen when their perspective is absent.

Blueprint of Roles - Checkout Flow

Role Involved	***Contribution***	***Risk if missed***
Product Owner	Aligns business requirements, customer expectations, and release priorities	Solution solves the wrong problem or misses key business needs
Frontend	Ensures UI reflects backend logic	Users see "Payment Successful" when transactions fail

QA	Identifies edge cases (failed payments, refunds, retries)	Refunds fail, customers wait, support tickets spike
Security	Reviews authentication, authorization, data protection, and payment security controls	Sensitive data exposure, fraud risk, compliance violations
DevOps	Sets up deployment pipelines, monitoring, rollback plans	Failures go undetected, recovery is slow

Pause and imagine: what happens if one of these conversations never takes place? A refund that cannot be processed, a UI that confuses users, or a compliance gap that blocks launch.

Without collaboration, you risk building a feature that looks polished but cracks under real-world use, like a house where the kitchen sink drains into the wrong pipe.

Think It Through

Collaboration is not abstract; it shows up in the cracks of real projects.

- When you picture the failed checkout launch, which missing collaboration step feels most familiar to your own work?
- How does your code ripple downstream into QA, frontend, DevOps, or product owners?
- Think about your last feature: did you invite input from QA, DevOps, or product before coding, or did you move ahead alone?
- If you had to explain collaboration to a non-technical friend, how would you use the house analogy to make it clear?
- What is one area in your current project where collaboration could prevent cracks before they appear?

Pause and reflect: these are not just questions; they are mirrors. Each answer reveals where your system is strong, and where silence might let cracks form.

From Reflection to Action

Pick a feature you are working on (or recently finished).

1. **List the roles involved**: QA, frontend, backend, DevOps, product owner, security, or any others.
2. **Write one sentence for each role**:
   – What do they need from me?
   – What do I need from them?
3. **Share your list with a teammate**: ask if they agree or spot missing connections.
4. **Reflect**: If one of these links broke, what failure story might unfold on launch day?

Think of this as drawing the blueprint of your "house." Every missing line is a pipe that will not connect or a wire that will not reach its outlet.

Collaboration is not just about preventing failure; it is about creating confidence. When teams share context, they build trust, clarity, and alignment that carry projects forward.

The checkout flow story shows how silence can unravel a launch, but the deeper lesson is this: **collaboration is the foundation. *It gives every teammate the clarity to act, the trust to rely on others, and the courage to face complexity together.***

And yet, even with collaboration, systems can still falter. That is where the debugging mindset begins, the focus of the next chapter.

Chapter 7: Debugging and Troubleshooting

Generative AI can help you write code quickly, but when things break and they will, it cannot debug your thinking. Your true value as a developer shows in how you respond when problems arise. Debugging is not just fixing errors; it is a mindset of curiosity, patience, and problem-solving.

It is late at night. You have just deployed a new feature. The dashboard glows green, the tests passed, and confidence feels high. Then the alerts start.

Users report they cannot log in. Error logs contradict each other. The database slows to a crawl. Your team chat lights up with questions: *"Is it the code? The config? The server?"*

In that moment, speed alone will not save you. Regenerating code blindly only adds confusion. **AI** can suggest hypotheses and potential fixes, but it cannot replace the investigation needed to understand why a problem occurred. What matters is how you think; whether you can stay calm, trace the issue, and uncover the root cause step by step.

Tracing the Cracks

Imagine living in a house where suddenly the lights flicker and go out, or water stops flowing. You do not demolish the house; you trace the wiring, check the fuse, or inspect the pipes. Debugging is the same: you do not throw away the system; you investigate step by step to find the root cause.

But sometimes the problem is not obvious. A flickering light might be a loose bulb, faulty wiring, or a tripped breaker. A damp wall could mean a leaking pipe, poor insulation, or even a clogged gutter outside. Troubleshooting is like being the house inspector: you walk through rooms, listen for drips, feel for dampness, and test switches until the hidden fault reveals itself.

Debugging requires the same mindset: patience to test each possibility, curiosity to explore hidden causes, and discipline to fix the source instead of covering up the symptoms.

Tracing the Fault Lines

Every symptom is a signal, but the real story lies beneath. Debugging means following those signals until you uncover the hidden fault lines that threaten the system.

Symptom (House/System)	***Possible Root Cause***	***Debugging Mindset***
Lights flicker	Loose bulb, faulty wiring, tripped breaker	Test each possibility step by step
Damp wall	Leaking pipe, poor insulation, clogged gutter	Trace the source instead of covering the stain

Slow login	Inefficient database query, misconfigured server, caching issue	Investigate logs, configs, and performance bottlenecks
Conflicting error messages	Multiple subsystems failing, inconsistent configs	Cross-check environments and isolate the failing component

Debugging is not limited to code. When a project stalls, when a conversation breaks down, or when a business process fails, the same mindset applies. Instead of rushing to patch symptoms, you pause, trace the root cause, and repair the system so it works again. *Debugging is ultimately a life skill*: curiosity to explore hidden causes, patience to test each possibility, and discipline to fix the source instead of painting over the cracks.

Signals of Debugging

These are not just technical terms; they are the signals you follow when systems falter. Each one is a clue, pointing you past the surface symptoms toward the deeper causes.

- **Root Cause**: The underlying reason a problem occurs, beyond surface symptoms.
- **Logs**: Recorded events or errors that help trace system behaviour.
- **Bottleneck**: A point in the system that slows down overall performance.

- **Troubleshooting**: The process of investigating and resolving issues step by step.
- **Reproduction**: The ability to consistently recreate an issue, making investigation and validation easier.

Together, these signals form the language of debugging: the trail you follow when clarity is hidden beneath confusion.

When Systems Falter

The dashboard glows green, tests pass, and confidence feels solid until the first support ticket arrives. You have just deployed a new login feature. Locally, everything worked fine. But once it hits production, the cracks appear:

- Some users cannot log in.
- Error logs show inconsistent messages.
- The database is responding slowly.
- Support tickets start piling up.
- Your team chat lights up: "Is it the code? The config? The server?"

Snippet thinking: Ask **AI** to regenerate the login code and redeploy.
Systems thinking:

- Check logs to trace the error path.
- Reproduce the issue with test accounts.
- Inspect database queries for performance bottlenecks.
- Collaborate with DevOps, QA, or other teammates to compare environments, reproduce the issue, and isolate the source of failure.

- Document the fix so future developers do not repeat the mistake.

Without a troubleshooting mindset, you risk patching symptoms instead of solving the actual problem, like painting over damp walls without fixing the leaking pipe.

Think It Through

Debugging is not just about fixing what is broken; it is about how you *think* when cracks appear.

- When something breaks, do you rush to rewrite code, or do you pause to investigate the system step by step?
- Think back to the last bug you solved. Did you uncover the underlying issue, or did you only patch the symptom?
- How do you usually trace an error: logs, test cases, peer discussion, or intuition? Which of these do you lean on most?
- If you had to explain debugging to a non-technical friend, how would you use the house analogy (flickering lights, damp walls) to make it relatable?
- Do you document your fixes so others can learn from them, or do you leave the knowledge locked in your own memory?

Reflect: *each answer is a mirror. It shows whether you patch cracks on the surface or trace them back to the fault lines beneath.*

From Reflection to Action

Pick a small feature you have built (like a search bar, API call, or login form).

1. **Break it on purpose**: introduce a wrong input, remove a dependency, or tweak a config so the feature fails.
2. **Trace the failure**: write down each step you take: checking logs, reproducing the bug, isolating the component.
3. **Compare approaches**: share your process with a peer. Notice where they start, what tools they use, and how their path differs from yours.
4. **Document the fix**: write instructions as if you were leaving a trail for the next developer. Make it clear enough that someone new could follow your steps and solve the issue.

Think of this as sketching the wiring diagram of your system. Every missing line is a wire that will not carry current, every broken link a pipe that will not connect.

The goal is not just to fix the bug, it is to practice the *mindset*: patience, curiosity, and clarity. Debugging is about leaving systems stronger than you found them. Every bug you solve is proof that you can face complexity and bring clarity. *Errors are opportunities to learn, not failures to hide.*

Carry this mindset beyond the prompt. Whether in code, projects, or life, *curiosity and patience* will always guide you to the root cause. And *with debugging mastered, you step into the bigger picture, a mindset that lasts beyond the snippet, beyond the system and into every challenge you face.*

Closing Thoughts

In this part, you have stepped into real-world readiness: the skills that make code usable beyond the sprint.

- **Thinking Beyond Code:** design for scalability, resilience, security, and observability.
- **Collaboration:** align with teammates so features connect seamlessly.
- **Debugging:** investigate root causes instead of patching symptoms.

Carry this forward: *treat readiness as ongoing care for systems.* ***AI*** *can generate code, but it cannot replace your mindset, teamwork, or problem-solving. With these habits, you stop being just a coder, you become the caretaker of systems, the builder of solutions, and the architect of trust.*

"Strong systems are not built by speed alone, but by care, clarity, and curiosity."

The journey does not end here. It expands into how you grow, how you lead, and how you build solutions that last. Readiness is not a destination; it is the foundation for leadership, resilience, and the confidence to meet complexity with clarity, purpose, and conviction as you navigate the challenges ahead.

Case Study: Order Report Export - Ticket to Production

Context: A new feature request arrives to *"Add a Download Report endpoint that returns CSV and PDF exports for order history, filtered by role and date range."*

Ticket & Acceptance Criteria

Criteria	*Details*
Audience	Admins (all orders), Users (own orders only)
Formats	CSV (streamed), PDF (async job)
Edge Cases	Empty results, large datasets, invalid date ranges
Dependencies	Orders database, PDF service, email provider
Observability	Request ID in logs, export duration metric, audit entry per export

Prompting AI (with checklist)

Before implementation, align with QA, security, and operations teams on test coverage, compliance requirements, monitoring expectations, and rollout strategy.

Prompt: "Generate a backend endpoint for GET /reports/orders with role-based filtering, pagination, streaming CSV response, async PDF job trigger using a background queue, request ID logging, audit logging, and export duration metrics. Include test stubs."

Checklist before accepting AI output:

- Permissions enforced
- Pagination included
- Audit logging present
- Metrics emitted
- Data masking for PII
- Security review

Component & Testing Strategy

Test Skeleton

```
Test: User sees only their own orders
- Setup: mock data source with mixed orders
- Execute: call report generation with user context
- Assert: output contains only user's orders

Test: Admin sees all orders
- Setup: mock data source with multiple users
- Execute: call report generation with admin context
- Assert: output includes all orders

Test: Empty results handled gracefully
- Setup: no matching orders
- Execute: call report generation
- Assert: output is valid CSV/PDF with headers only
```

Test Plan:

- Role-based access (admin vs user)
- Empty results return valid CSV headers

- ➢ Large dataset streaming (simulate 100k rows)
- ➢ PDF provider timeout → fallback queue
- ➢ Database slow query → latency alert triggered

Non-Functional Checks

Dimension	*What to Verify*
Scalability	Streaming CSV, pagination, async PDF jobs
Resilience	Timeouts, retries with backoff, circuit breaker for PDF provider
Performance	p95 latency < 2s, error rate < 1%
Security	Role filtering enforced, PII masking validated, audit trail generated
Monitoring	Logs with request id, metrics (duration, rows returned, queue depth)
Alerting	p95 > 2000ms for 5m → P1; error rate > 1% for 5m → P1
Maintainability	Clear interfaces, API contract docs, runbook link in pull request

CI/CD Pipeline

Flow Diagram (textual):

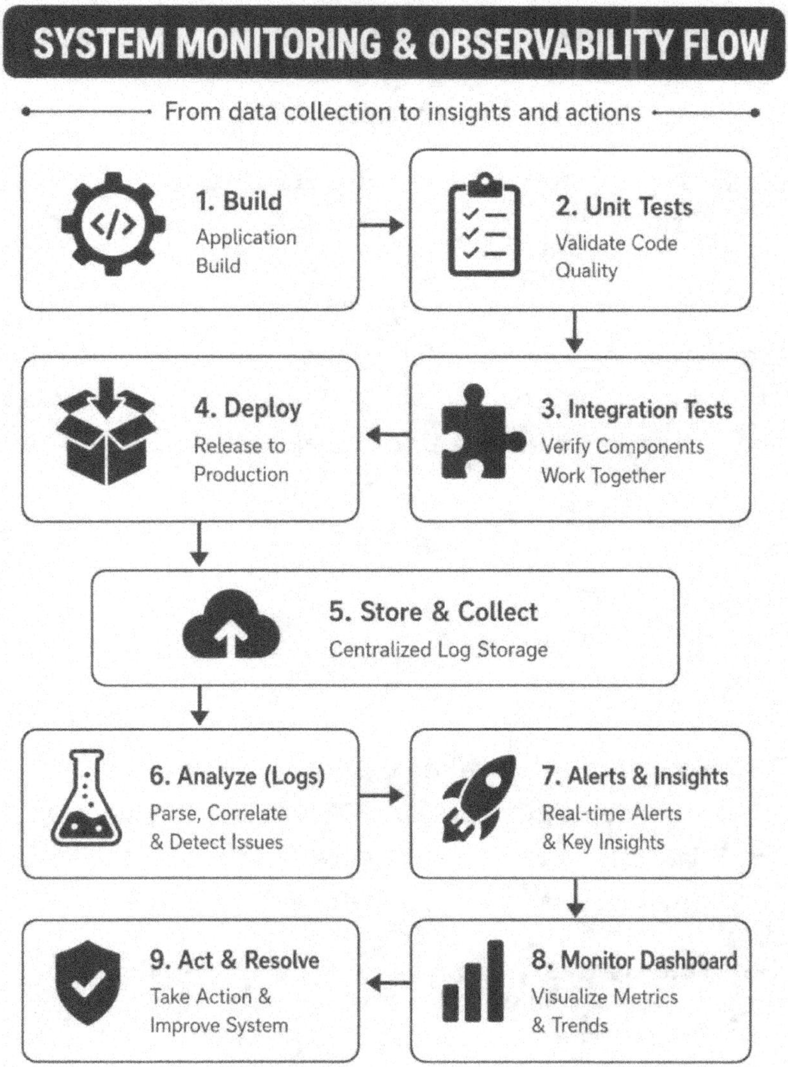

Deployment Checklist:

- Canary rollout to a small percentage of users before full release
- Feature flag for quick disable
- Rollback plan (previous artifact)
- Smoke tests: role-based access, CSV/PDF export

Post-Deployment Monitoring & Runbook

Immediate checks (first 30m):

If any metric degrades unexpectedly, begin troubleshooting by reproducing the issue, tracing logs with request IDs, and isolating whether the problem originates in the application, database, or external providers.

- p95 latency
- Error rate
- Queue depth
- PDF provider success rate

Runbook Template:

- **Detect:** Alert triggers (latency, error rate, queue depth)
- **Isolate:** Identify database vs PDF provider vs code issue
- **Mitigate:** Fallback queue, feature flag disables, rollback
- **Learn:** Add missing tests, update docs, assign owner

Key Takeaways

- Prompts accelerate code generation, but **checklists ensure completeness**.

- **Tests and nonfunctional checks** make features production-ready.
- **CI/CD safeguards** (canary, rollback, feature flags) protect users.
- **Runbooks and monitoring** turn incidents into learning opportunities.

The case study showed how a single feature, the Order Report export, travels from ticket to production. But as developers, our responsibility does not end when code is merged. Systems live on, and they fail in ways we must anticipate. That is where a runbook comes in.

The case study shows how we build thoughtfully. The runbook carries that thinking into production, helping teams detect issues, isolate causes, mitigate quickly, and learn for the future. Together, they form two sides of the same coin: ***the mindset and the operational discipline that make us not just coders, but caretakers of systems***.

Carry this forward*: every feature you ship is not just code, but trust. And every system you care for is proof that you build solutions that last.*

Runbook: Order Report Export

Detect	Isolate
➢ Run smoke test (admin + user export) ➢ Check dashboards (latency, error rate, queue depth) ➢ Confirm scope (global vs local issue, recent deploys)	➢ Inspect logs/traces for failing request IDs ➢ Analyse database queries for bottlenecks ➢ Check external provider status (PDF/email)
Mitigate	**Learn**
➢ Toggle feature flag to disable exports. ➢ Rollback last deploy if metrics do not stabilize. ➢ Enqueue fallback jobs or switch to cached path.	➢ Conduct incident review within 24 hours ➢ Capture lessons in documentation ➢ Share fixes and improvements with the team.

Acceptance Checklist

Functional

- CSV/PDF formats
- Role-filtered results
- Pagination/streaming

Security

- Role checks enforced
- PII masking/redaction

- Rate limits applied

Edge Cases

- Empty results handled
- Large export sets supported
- Invalid dates rejected

Non-functional

- Latency monitored
- Error rate tracked
- Queue depth observed

Testing

- Unit & integration tests
- Smoke & load tests

Deployment

- Feature flag gating
- Canary rollout (10%)
- Rollback plan read

Final Thoughts: Beyond the Prompt

"You have completed this guide, but in truth, this is only the beginning of your journey as a developer."

We began with mindset, learning that prompts can give you bricks, but only you can design the house. We moved into process, understanding the Software Development Life Cycle as the blueprint that keeps the house strong. And we ended with practice, thinking beyond code, collaborating with others, and developing the patience to debug and repair when things go wrong.

Together, these lessons remind us that software development is not about how quickly code is produced. It is about how effectively we connect the dots, anticipate ripple effects, and build systems that stand the test of time.

The house analogy lives on:

- You are the ***architect*** who sees the bigger picture.
- You are the ***builder*** who follows the blueprint.
- You are the ***caretaker*** who maintains, adapts, and strengthens the house over time.

The most important lesson in this book is not a framework, a checklist, or a prompt. It is the habit of pausing long enough to think before acting. Tools will continue to change. Technologies will continue to evolve. The developers who thrive are the ones who learn how to connect decisions, systems, and outcomes.

AI tools will continue to evolve, but your mindset, collaboration, judgment, and problem-solving are what make you valuable. Your career grows not by prompting faster, but by thinking deeper, designing smarter, and taking responsibility for the solutions you build.

***Carry this forward**: every feature you build is a brick in a larger house. Make it strong. Make it purposeful. Make it last.*

Technology will continue to change, but thoughtful design, collaboration, and systems thinking will remain the foundations of solutions that endure.

*Thank you for reading, and I hope this book helps you build solutions that **last beyond the prompt**.*

About the Author

Nidhi Mehra is a backend engineer with more than a decade of experience building scalable systems and solving complex engineering challenges.

She works across backend platforms, workflow automation, cloud services, database integrations, and enterprise applications. Her work has focused on designing and delivering reliable software solutions that perform effectively under real-world constraints such as scale, performance, maintainability, and operational complexity.

As a technical lead, she has spent years supporting and guiding early-career developers within project teams. Over time, she noticed a recurring pattern: many developers could learn frameworks, tools, and even AI-assisted coding techniques, yet often struggled to understand the broader systems, processes, and decisions required to deliver successful software solutions.

She realized that many of these lessons were being shared only within project teams, while a much wider audience could benefit from them.

Through ***Beyond the Prompt: Building Real Solutions in the Age of AI***, Nidhi shares practical lessons drawn from real-world software development, encouraging developers to combine AI-assisted productivity with systems thinking, sound decision-making, collaboration, and professional responsibility.

Her goal is simple: to help developers build solutions that work not only in code editors, but also in production, and ultimately build solutions that ***last beyond the prompt***.

If these ideas sparked new ways of thinking, I would love to hear your reflections. Connect with me on LinkedIn at www.linkedIn.com/in/nidhi-mehra-anand or follow along for future volumes. Together, we will keep building systems that last.

BEYOND PROMPTS LIES PURPOSE.

BEYOND CODE LIES IMPACT.

www.ingramcontent.com/pod-product-compliance
Lightning Source LLC
LaVergne TN
LVHW022228200926
848481LV00006B/2171

* 9 7 9 8 9 0 6 0 6 0 6 1 7 *